5 STEPS TO A ➤ 5

500
AP* World History Questions
to know by test day

Also in the 5 Steps Series:
5 Steps to a 5: AP World History
5 Steps to a 5: AP World History with CD-ROM
5 Steps to a 5: AP World History Flashcards
5 Steps to a 5: AP World History Flashcards for Your iPod
5 Steps to a 5: AP World History (iPhone App)

Also in the 500 AP Questions to Know by Test Day series:
5 Steps to a 5: 500 AP English Language Questions to Know by Test Day
5 Steps to a 5: 500 AP English Literature Questions to Know by Test Day
5 Steps to a 5: 500 AP Biology Questions to Know by Test Day
5 Steps to a 5: 500 AP Psychology Questions to Know by Test Day
5 Steps to a 5: 500 AP U.S. History Questions to Know by Test Day

5 STEPS TO A >5™

500
AP* World History Questions
to know by test day

Adam Stevens

New York   Chicago   San Francisco   Athens   London   Madrid
Mexico City   Milan   New Delhi   Singapore   Sydney   Toronto

6 7 8 9 10 11 12 13 14 15 16 17 18   QFR/QFR   1 0 9 8 7 6 5

ISBN   978-0-07-174209-2
MHID   0-07-174209-3

e-ISBN   978-0-07-174210-8
e-MHID   0-07-174210-7

Library of Congress Control Number   2010935990

Series interior design by Jane Tenenbaum

McGraw-Hill Education products are available at special quantity discounts to use as premiums and sales promotions or for use in corporate training programs. To contact a representative, please visit the Contact Us pages at www.mhprofessional.com.

This book is printed on acid-free paper.

CONTENTS

ABOUT THE AUTHOR

Adam Stevens graduated from Columbia University with a BA in history in 1996. He is currently a teacher living in Brooklyn with his wife, Helena, and his two children, Omar and Alexandra.

INTRODUCTION

Congratulations! You've taken a big step toward AP success by purchasing *5 Steps to a 5: 500 AP World History Questions to Know by Test Day*. We are here to help you take the next step and score high on your AP Exam so you can earn college credits and get into the college or university of your choice!

This book gives you 500 AP-style multiple-choice questions that cover all the most essential course material. Each question has a detailed answer explanation. These questions will give you valuable independent practice to supplement your regular textbook and the groundwork you are already doing in your AP classroom.

This and the other books in this series were written by expert AP teachers who know your exam inside out and can identify the crucial exam information as well as questions that are most likely to appear on the exam.

You might be the kind of student who takes several AP courses and needs to study extra questions a few weeks before the exam for a final review. Or you might be the kind of student who puts off preparing until the last weeks before the exam. No matter what your preparation style, you will surely benefit from reviewing these 500 questions, which closely parallel the content, format, and degree of difficulty of the questions on the actual AP exam. These questions and their answer explanations are the ideal last-minute study tool for those final few weeks before the test.

Remember the old saying "Practice makes perfect." If you practice with all the questions and answers in this book, we are certain you will build the skills and confidence needed to do great on the exam. Good luck!

—Editors of McGraw-Hill Education

CHAPTER 1

Foundations: 8000 BCE to 600 CE

Controlling Idea

In the Foundations unit basic patterns of human interaction that we adhere to in today's world arise. For the first time, with the origins of agriculture, humans were able to consistently generate food on a scale beyond what was needed by the individual producer to survive. This surplus production, and various social and political arrangements constructed to regulate its distribution in human populations, is the fundamental point of departure in AP World History. Class society, a society of laborers and owners (with diverse subdivisions of these two major groups), emerged in each center of civilization shaped how this surplus was to be shared. The move to ownership disproportionately enriched males and so we see the origins of patriarchy in the Foundations era as well. Finally, religions and belief systems that shape the worldviews of billions today can be traced to this period of history, the Foundations era.

1. Which of the following was NOT a common trait of early civilizations?

   (A) Writing
   (B) Formal state structures
   (C) Urban life
   (D) Monument building
   (E) Nomadism

2. Where did the earliest civilizations tend to develop?

   (A) Mountain plateaus
   (B) Coastlines
   (C) River valleys
   (D) Grassland steppes
   (E) Archipelagoes

3. Based on the preponderance of archaeological evidence, which region of the world saw the development of the earliest civilizations?
   (A) Northern Eurasia
   (B) South America
   (C) Indonesia
   (D) The Middle East
   (E) North America

4. Which people are generally credited with founding Mesopotamian civilization in the Tigris-Euphrates river valley?
   (A) Akkadians
   (B) Hittites
   (C) Sumerians
   (D) Greeks
   (E) Phoenicians

5. What conclusions can we draw about Babylonian society from the following excerpt from Hammurabi's Code?

221. If a physician heals the broken bone or diseased soft part of a man, the patient shall pay the physician five shekels in money. 222. If he were a freed man he shall pay three shekels. 223. If he were a slave his owner shall pay the physician two shekels.

   (A) Babylonian medical practice was informed by study of microscopic germs.
   (B) Babylonian physicians attended formal medical school for many years of training similar to doctors today.
   (C) Babylonian physicians healed most cases of broken bones in Mesopotamia.
   (D) Babylonian medical practice reflected prevailing patterns in social status.
   (E) Babylonian doctors heeded the Hippocratic oath.

6. Which of the following is NOT true of the ancient Egyptian pyramids?
   (A) Served as tombs for pharaohs
   (B) Were built by slave and corvee labor
   (C) Are reflective of advanced geometric knowledge
   (D) Contained numerous hieroglyphic symbols
   (E) Were built under the influence of Chinese advisors

7. Which of the following early river valley civilizations developed in the greatest state of isolation from the others?

   (A) Tigris River
   (B) Euphrates River
   (C) Indus River
   (D) Huang He River
   (E) Nile River

8. Which people are credited with developing the first phonetic alphabet?

   (A) Egyptians
   (B) Sumerians
   (C) Phoenicians
   (D) Chinese
   (E) Koreans

9. Which choice best characterizes the relationship between early civilizations and writing?

   (A) Writing permitted record keeping for trade and governments.
   (B) Writing led to the development of civilization more than sedentary agriculture.
   (C) Most civilizations developed without writing systems.
   (D) No sophisticated civilization developed without a system of writing.
   (E) There is no important relationship between civilization and writing.

10. Which of the following was true for ALL of the early agricultural systems?

   (A) Domestication of perennial plants in each region
   (B) Wheat and barley cultivation
   (C) Economic activity based on raising a combination of domesticated plants and draft animals
   (D) Primary reliance on pastoral forms of social organization
   (E) Abandonment of sedentary agriculture

11. Which statement is most accurate regarding Jewish monotheism?

   (A) It traces its origins to Abraham.
   (B) It was spread by missionaries in the Ganges River valley.
   (C) It appealed mainly to wealthier people.
   (D) It incorporated the idea of reincarnation.
   (E) It rejected all of the laws of the Mesopotamian civilization.

12. Confucianism, Hinduism, and Christianity had what in common?
    (A) They directed attention to the afterlife.
    (B) They helped justify and preserve social inequality.
    (C) They urged the importance of political activity.
    (D) They stressed the value of warfare.
    (E) They incorporated a strong missionary drive.

13. Which of the following did ancient Egyptian, Shang, and Sumerian civilizations all have in common?
    (A) Pyramid-shaped monumental architecture
    (B) River valley location
    (C) Acceptance of Buddhism
    (D) Pastoral-based economy
    (E) Intensive rice agriculture

14. The period 8000 BCE to 600 CE saw all of the following EXCEPT
    (A) Birth of major world religions
    (B) Origin of agriculture
    (C) Use of gunpowder
    (D) Urbanization
    (E) Development of writing

15. Which of the following classical societies was based in the eastern Mediterranean Sea?
    (A) Greek
    (B) Mauryan
    (C) Han
    (D) Gupta
    (E) Mayan

16. River valley civilizations, such as the Egyptians or Sumerians, developed all of the following EXCEPT
    (A) Craft specialization
    (B) Social stratification
    (C) Constitutional monarchy
    (D) Long-distance trade
    (E) Complex religious rituals

17. Which ancient civilization fits the description found below?
    - Constructed multistory structures
    - Arose near the Indus River
    - Disappeared for reasons that remain unclear

    (A) Harappan
    (B) Shang
    (C) Kushite
    (D) Mayan
    (E) Mauryan

18. Which civilization's decline was most likely due to drastic environmental change?

    (A) Indus
    (B) Han
    (C) Roman
    (D) Egyptian
    (E) Assyrian

19. Which example from the classical world best characterizes the principle of cultural diffusion?

    (A) Preference for silk garments among the Roman elite
    (B) Victory of Sparta in the Peloponnesian War
    (C) Conversion of Asoka to Buddhism
    (D) Growing influence of Confucianism in China during the Han dynasty
    (E) Sacking of Rome by the Visigoths in 410 CE

20. All of the following were important impacts of the rise of metalwork in the ancient world EXCEPT:

    (A) Metal tools make farming easier.
    (B) Metal arms revolutionized war fighting.
    (C) Specialized labor developed further.
    (D) Metal ships revolutionized trade and naval warfare.
    (E) Metallic coins facilitated trade.

21. What additional challenge do historians studying the Harappan civilization of the Indus River valley face that does not exist when studying Sumerian or Egyptian civilizations?

    (A) Artifacts lie under layers of earth that must be carefully excavated by archaeologists.
    (B) Religious prohibitions on interfering with the burial places of the Hindu dead slow excavation projects.
    (C) Historians rely entirely on legends and oral history as no archaeological record of Harappan civilization exists.
    (D) Harappan writing has never been deciphered.
    (E) Political instability in the Indus River valley in the modern era has made sustained archaeological research impossible.

22. Which is the name of the ancient Sumerian writing system?

    (A) Hieroglyphics
    (B) Ideograph
    (C) Pictograph
    (D) Cuneiform
    (E) Phonetics

23. The order in which these empires or civilizations emerged was
    I. Sumerian
    II. Shang
    III. Roman
    IV. Han

    (A) I, II, III, IV
    (B) I, II, IV, III
    (C) II, I, IV, III
    (D) II, III, I, IV
    (E) IV, III, II, I

24. Based on available knowledge, which of the following was NOT a part of *Homo erectus'* world?

    (A) Tool making
    (B) Language
    (C) Bipedalism
    (D) Hunting
    (E) Agriculture

25. Compared to other revolutions in world history, which feature of the Neolithic Revolution is most unusual?

   (A) Altered gender roles and relations
   (B) Attenuated unfolding over thousands of years in diverse locales
   (C) Impact on population growth
   (D) Transformation of class relations
   (E) Abandonment of previously held patterns of religious worship

26. Which set of Paleolithic practices would prove most durable as humans entered the Neolithic era?

   (A) Generally egalitarian principles of social organization
   (B) Metallurgical expertise
   (C) Domestication of animals
   (D) Nomadic lifestyle
   (E) Hunting of wild big-game mammals as a major source of protein

27. Which of the following was NOT a unique advantage agricultural people enjoyed over hunter-gatherer groups as a sedentary lifestyle began to confront nomadic lifestyles after 8000 BCE?

   (A) Immunities built up to new diseases spawned in denser nodes of population
   (B) Regular armed forces capable of sustained offensive and defensive campaigns
   (C) Greater ability to store food in preparation for times of scarcity
   (D) Higher levels of social equality and group cohesion
   (E) Tools and weapons made of metal

28. In what respects did pastoralism lay important foundations for subsequent stages of human development?

   (A) Human societies first began to follow the leadership of recognized spiritual guides.
   (B) Domesticated mammals began to provide more consistent sources of hides, bone, and protein.
   (C) Groups learned how to select seeds and grains that over time yielded more bountiful harvests.
   (D) Settled living formed the basis for early writing systems.
   (E) The American continents were first populated by pastoral peoples.

29. Which of the following early crops was unique to the early civilizations of what would later be termed the New World?
    (A) Oats
    (B) Millet
    (C) Barley
    (D) Wheat
    (E) Maize

30. What best characterizes the evolving role of women as human society moved from preagricultural to agricultural modes of production?
    (A) Tending to large flocks of domesticated animals
    (B) Foraging and fashioning stone tools
    (C) Having greater confinement to the home to care for more numerous children
    (D) Spending most time at the market to trade the family's surplus farm goods
    (E) Guiding religious worship in village or town temples

31. Which of the following best describes the development of agriculture during the Neolithic era?
    (A) It was a gradual process, arising independently in diverse regions and climatic conditions on the globe.
    (B) It spread from the Americas across a land bridge to Asia and then to Europe.
    (C) It was limited to China until the first millennium BCE.
    (D) It was practiced only on hilly terrain.
    (E) It generally brought on lower population densities in the areas to which it spread.

32. What economic effect did food surpluses have on early agricultural societies?
    (A) Hunting animals was eliminated as a source of food.
    (B) A social hierarchy developed with peasants on the top.
    (C) The first long-distance trade networks were established.
    (D) People abandoned all other trades to become farmers.
    (E) Trade practices emerged with the capacity to feed artisans who then had time to practice craft specialization.

33. What, in general, was the health impact as human populations abandoned nomadism and settled into a sedentary agricultural lifestyle?

(A) Rates of parasitic diseases were reduced.

(B) Greater exposure to pathogens due to proximity to farm animals and human waste caused new sicknesses.

(C) Disease rates fell due to the vigorous lifestyle of hard labor.

(D) Nutrition generally improved, resulting from the greater diversity of foodstuffs the laboring peasantry had to choose from.

(E) Overall health improved as new governments made provision of universal health care a top priority.

34. Which of the following is associated with the "Out of Africa" thesis on human origins?

 I. Origin of anatomically modern humans in Africa

 II. Separate origins of anatomically modern humans across the Old World

 III. Evolution of *Homo neanderthalensis* into *Homo sapiens*

(A) I and III

(B) II only

(C) II and III

(D) I and II

(E) I only

35. Broadly speaking, which choice places the developments associated with the Neolithic Revolution in the correct chronological order?

(A) Specialization of labor, social stratification, surplus food production

(B) Surplus food production, specialization of labor, social stratification

(C) Social stratification, specialization of labor, surplus food production

(D) Specialization of labor, surplus food production, social stratification

(E) Surplus food production, social stratification, specialization of labor

36. Which of the following is the least intensive and sophisticated agricultural practice?

(A) Use of chemical fertilizer

(B) Irrigation

(C) Terrace farming

(D) Slash and burn

(E) Three-field system

37. The preponderance of evidence would suggest that human settlement reached which of the following regions most recently?
    (A) Australia
    (B) South America
    (C) Scandinavia
    (D) India
    (E) South Africa

38. Which region of the world had yet to experience the Neolithic transition by 600 CE?
    (A) Mesoamerica
    (B) South America
    (C) Northern Europe
    (D) Australia
    (E) Southeast Asia

39. The label "Paleolithic" sometimes serves as a substitute for which of the following?
    I. Bronze Age
    II. Iron Age
    III. Stone Age

    (A) I and II
    (B) II and III
    (C) I and III
    (D) I only
    (E) III only

40. Hellenistic culture epitomizes which of the following historical forces or trends?
    (A) Isolationism
    (B) Cultural diffusion
    (C) Patriarchy
    (D) Egalitarianism
    (E) Democracy

41. Hellenistic culture brought together the traditions of which of the following regions?
    (A) Mediterranean, Mesoamerican, sub-Saharan African
    (B) Middle Eastern, Mediterranean, Scandinavian
    (C) Mesoamerican, Scandinavian, Mediterranean
    (D) East Asian, South Asian, sub-Saharan African
    (E) Middle Eastern, Mediterranean, South Asian

42. Which of the following political practices remained continuous from the period of the Republic into the period of the Roman Empire?

(A) Strict rules separating military service and political leadership
(B) Dominant involvement of the plebian classes in state affairs
(C) Primacy placed in a Senate where state affairs were debated
(D) Imperial military assistance for slave uprisings
(E) Recruitment of local elites in recently conquered areas to represent the interests of the imperial center

43. Which of the following prominent Greeks exercised practical political leadership?

(A) Aristotle
(B) Solon
(C) Plato
(D) Socrates
(E) Euripides

44. Which choice best describes the position of women in classical Athens in terms of divorce and property rights as compared to women in classical Roman society? Greek women had

(A) Far greater rights
(B) Somewhat greater rights
(C) About the same level of rights
(D) Somewhat fewer rights
(E) Far fewer rights

45. Which of the following pairings most accurately reflects existing trade connections in the Greco-Roman era?

(A) Han-Roman
(B) Scandinavian-Greek
(C) Polynesian-Roman
(D) Gupta-Greek
(E) Olmec-Greek

46. Which prominent Greek individual listed below was not part of a direct teacher-student relationship shared by the other four?

(A) Alexander the Great
(B) Socrates
(C) Aristotle
(D) Herodotus
(E) Plato

47. Which of the following best describes BOTH the Roman and the Han empires?

    (A) Neither empire was linked to the Silk Roads.
    (B) Both empires used the family as the model for state organization.
    (C) Mounting costs associated with defending imperial frontiers led to economic and political crises.
    (D) New religions were easily assimilated into existing imperial religious ideologies.
    (E) Taxation of mercantile activity accounted for most government revenue.

48. What was a common feature of classical civilizations in India, China, and the Mediterranean?

    (A) Agricultural systems dependent on monsoon rains
    (B) Social hierarchy
    (C) Absence of coerced labor
    (D) Elimination of patriarchy over time
    (E) Maintenance of highly centralized governments throughout the entire classical period 1000 BCE to 600 CE

49. What similarity did early Buddhism and early Christianity share?

    (A) Support for caste hierarchy
    (B) Requirement of total celibacy for men
    (C) Allowance of women to enter monastic life
    (D) Inclusion of Greek and Roman gods into their pantheon
    (E) Prohibition of conversion

50. Which pair of rulers underwent a religious conversion process that had a broad-based impact on the lands under their control?

    (A) Julius Caesar and Shi Huangdi
    (B) Hammurabi and Julius Caesar
    (C) Tutankhamen and Pericles
    (D) Asoka and Constantine
    (E) Henry VIII and Justinian

51. Which policy did both Roman and Han armies tend to implement upon taking control of a foreign land?

(A) Enslavement of the entire working-age population

(B) Repression of local worship and imposition of a state religion

(C) Cessation of trade contact with the rest of the world

(D) Construction of libraries and universities

(E) Relative autonomy for cooperative local elites

52. Before 600 CE, nomadic peoples of the Eurasian landmass

(A) Lived in a state of constant warfare with neighboring civilizations

(B) Were dependent on the camel for covering large distances

(C) Maintained strict isolation from nearby civilizations

(D) Interacted intermittently with civilizations, often through trade

(E) Continuously moved farther from civilizations into high mountain, sub-Arctic, and Arctic zones

53. Why did the western portion of the Roman Empire suffer so much more in the breakdown of Roman imperial unity than the regions of the Eastern Roman Empire (Byzantium)?

(A) The feudal system in the west relied on a trade system made unreliable by harsh winters.

(B) The Eastern Roman world had traditionally been more economically vibrant due to more active trade links with the East.

(C) Popes of the Roman Catholic church maintained harmonious relations with western feudal lords.

(D) The Eastern Orthodox church attracted more followers than the Roman church.

(E) Germanic peoples migrated to Byzantium after fleeing nomadic attackers.

54. Which of the following is the most accurate statement about ancient Roman trade routes?

(A) On every trade route enslaved persons were the chief commodity being transported.

(B) Western Europe was the most profitable trade destination of the empire and had the most trade routes.

(C) Most trade routes were focused around the Mediterranean Sea.

(D) The Silk Road was Rome's most important trade route.

(E) Roman ships dominated the trade of the Indian Ocean.

55. Which weakness of the Roman Empire contributed most directly to its collapse?

   (A) It was too vast to impose unity and order among all of the regions.
   (B) Mountain ranges blocked effective transport and communications between key areas.
   (C) It was too small to marshal resources necessary to protect itself from rival powers.
   (D) Repeated incursions into the territories of powerful empires to the east resulted in devastating offensives.
   (E) It did not have access to waterways suitable for carrying out long-distance trade.

56. After the fall of Rome, the eastern half of the empire became renamed the

   (A) Holy Roman Empire
   (B) Bactrian Empire
   (C) Byzantine Empire
   (D) Visigoth Kingdom
   (E) Vandalistan

57. Which of the following civilizations afforded the greatest degree of citizen input into government policy?

   (A) Han
   (B) Roman
   (C) Sumerian
   (D) Egyptian
   (E) Gupta

58. In Greek civilization, women

   (A) Held slave status in every household
   (B) Enjoyed political equality with men
   (C) Were afforded the same rights no matter the city-state in which they happened to reside
   (D) Dominated trade
   (E) Were considered inferior to men in both the private and public spheres

59. Christianity's rise is most accurately viewed as a modification of which of the following?

(A) Islam
(B) Hinduism
(C) Judaism
(D) Confucianism
(E) Buddhism

60. Which of the following terms is NOT associated with classical Greek architecture?

(A) Doric
(B) Ionic
(C) Corinthian
(D) Parthenon
(E) Ziggurat

61. Which neighboring power posed the greatest military threat over the course of classical Greek civilization?

(A) Egyptian
(B) Mongol
(C) Persian
(D) Balkan
(E) Islamic

62. The geographic factors presented here led to the development of which highly complex and distinctive civilization by the year 600 CE?

- Fertile river valleys
- Isolating mountain ranges
- Dependable monsoon weather patterns

(A) Indian
(B) Roman
(C) Mayan
(D) Sumerian
(E) Greek

63. Which of the following best describes political patterns on the Indian subcontinent in the classical era 1000 BCE to 600 CE?

   (A) Stateless societies
   (B) Continuous dynastic rule under the Maurya Empire
   (C) Decentralized rule by local princes lacking any form of subcontinent-wide authority at any point
   (D) Decentralized rule by local princes punctuated by Maurya and Gupta periods of unification
   (E) Representative democracy

64. Which was the most effective unifying force in early Indian culture?

   (A) Long-distance trade with East Asian civilizations
   (B) Widely practiced and similar Hindu tradition, including the caste system
   (C) Expansion of Buddhist influence
   (D) Recognized central political authority
   (E) Matriarchal patterns of social authority

65. Which of the following is unique to the Hindu religion when compared to other major world religions?

   I. Belief in some form of afterlife
   II. Absence of a central founding figure
   III. Distinct denominations

   (A) I only
   (B) II only
   (C) I and II
   (D) II and III
   (E) I, II, and III

66. Which major world religion lacks a central founding figure?

   (A) Christianity
   (B) Islam
   (C) Judaism
   (D) Buddhism
   (E) Hinduism

67. Which is NOT a significant continuity Buddhism carried over from its Hindu roots?

   (A) Endorsement of caste stratification
   (B) Belief in an afterlife
   (C) Concern with and reverence for beauty in nature
   (D) Ornate temple architecture
   (E) Centrality of ritual in worship

68. How did the Hindu doctrine of dharma impact Indian society?

   (A) It fostered the formation of rigid social and economic groups.
   (B) It was the basis of equality under the law between men and women.
   (C) It influenced the priestly class to implement a standardized set of religious rituals for Hindus.
   (D) It initiated an integrated economic system to aid merchants.
   (E) It caused the majority of the subcontinent's population to settle near the holy waters of the Ganges River.

69. Which of the following ancient texts did not serve as a spiritual guide to salvation for those who lived by it?

   (A) Vedas
   (B) Analects
   (C) Torah
   (D) New Testament of the Bible
   (E) Koran

70. Which important idea is credited to intellectuals of the Gupta Empire?

   (A) Invention of the telescope
   (B) Development of humanity's first written script
   (C) The concept of zero
   (D) Invention of the magnetic compass
   (E) Polytheism

71. Which beliefs do Hinduism and Buddhism have in common?

   (A) Belief in the caste system
   (B) Damnation for sinners
   (C) Reverence for Muhammad
   (D) Monotheism
   (E) Reincarnation

72. Which lasting pattern in the history of the subcontinent can we trace to the period of the rule of the Maurya and Gupta empires in India?
    (A) Strong state sponsorship of Hindu beliefs
    (B) Invasion and rule by nomadic invaders
    (C) Difficulty in maintaining centralized imperial rule
    (D) Long and generally unbroken eras of centralized imperial rule
    (E) Coexistence with Islamic rule and culture

73. Why did long-distance trade flourish in the classical world?
    (A) Stable imperial authority provided safe passage for merchants.
    (B) Circumnavigation of the globe by the Romans increased access to goods from distant lands.
    (C) Silk Roads were so safe that individual traders frequently traveled their entire distance.
    (D) Stable central rule in India throughout the period made it a vital hub of trade.
    (E) Bantu migrations helped establish a common linguistic bond across the Eurasian landmass.

74. Buddhism's rise is most accurately viewed as a modification of which of the following belief systems?
    (A) Confucianism
    (B) Islam
    (C) Christianity
    (D) Daoism
    (E) Hinduism

75. Which of the following regions does NOT belong in a list of lands to which Buddhism spread substantially in the centuries following the death of Siddhartha Gautama?
    (A) Southeast Asia
    (B) Mesopotamia
    (C) China
    (D) Japan
    (E) Central Asia

76. Which is the best estimate for the number of castes that have developed in India over the millennia?

(A) A handful
(B) Dozens
(C) Hundreds
(D) Thousands
(E) Billions

77. Which of the following texts contain major religious documents that originated in India?

  I. Vedas
 II. Bhagavad Gita
III. Koran

(A) I and II
(B) II and III
(C) I, II, and III
(D) I only
(E) III only

78. Which statement comparing classical Chinese civilization with contemporary Western civilization is most accurate?

(A) The Chinese economy relied on slavery to a greater extent than Western civilization did.
(B) China set an enduring pattern of more sophisticated agricultural, metallurgical, and textile production techniques than Western civilization.
(C) Women had markedly greater maneuverability within Chinese civilization to achieve positions of high social status.
(D) The Chinese developed a simplified phonetic writing system similar to Hebrew.
(E) In China agriculture was replaced by handicraft manufacturing as the main economic base of society.

79. Which of the following was NOT a tactic used by Shi Huangdi to unify China into one empire?

(A) Relying mainly on diplomacy and not military force to achieve territorial expansion
(B) Appointing bureaucrats to rule the provinces, displacing regional aristocrats
(C) Building the Great Wall to guard against invasion
(D) Establishing uniform currency and measurements
(E) Employing legalism as the state political philosophy

80. Which choice best captures the main difference between legalist and Confucian beliefs?

(A) Legalism relied on harsh laws to maintain order while Confucianism depended on rituals, customs, and obligations rooted in family relations.

(B) Legalism never became state doctrine while Confucianism did under the Han dynasty.

(C) Confucianism never became state doctrine while legalism did under the Qin dynasty.

(D) Legalism's complex formulas for achieving spiritual enlightenment took greater root among the masses than the Confucian emphasis on achieving inner peace through unity with the natural world.

(E) Legalism emphasized egalitarian class relations while Confucianism was more concerned with maintaining established hierarchies.

81. Which of the following was NOT a lasting feature of Chinese civilization formed by the later Zhou era?

(A) Origin and early spread of a Daoist worldview

(B) Dynastic rule and the conception of the Mandate of Heaven

(C) Intensive river valley irrigation and agriculture

(D) Confucian social prescriptions to guide family and state-subject relations

(E) Significant Buddhist penetration and influence among the broad masses of the people

82. With which early Chinese emperors and dynasties do we most closely associate non-Confucian worldviews?

  I. Wu Ti of the Han dynasty

  II. Shi Huangdi of the Qin dynasty

  III. Empress Wu of the Tang dynasty

(A) I and II

(B) II and III

(C) I and III

(D) I only

(E) II only

83. Confucian thought falls most neatly into which of the following categories?
    (A) Conservative political philosophy aiming to preserve a hierarchical status quo
    (B) Prophetic millennial ideology preparing the masses for an impending judgment day
    (C) Spiritual guide to gaining salvation for the individual's eternal soul
    (D) Revolutionary ideology aimed at dismantling social hierarchy
    (E) Set of moral precepts designed to promote a more harmonious union between man and nature

84. Which of the following was NOT an important basis for the higher socioeconomic status of the Chinese gentry?
    (A) Control or ownership of extensive farmland
    (B) Ability to afford preparation of gentry youth for civil service exams
    (C) Durable positions as local tax collectors and intermediaries for the imperial center
    (D) Commonplace advancement of women of the gentry class in the imperial bureaucracy
    (E) Ability to call in military resources of the imperial state to put down local peasant rebellions

85. Which of the following best describes how Chinese imperial elites viewed their civilization in relation to the rest of the world?
    (A) China was a unique and superior civilization surrounded by barbarians of one sort or another.
    (B) China was an intermediary civilization whose main role was to facilitate the exchange of trade items and ideas between surrounding and more advanced societies.
    (C) China was one member of a peer group of advanced civilizations.
    (D) China was a great civilization trapped in an irreversible decline due to nomadic invasion and inability to support massive population growth.
    (E) China was a rising civilization learning from and preparing to overtake existing world powers.

86. Which of the following qualifies as an example of Confucius's "Five Basic Relationships"?
    (A) Ruler-subject
    (B) Father-son
    (C) Friend-friend
    (D) Husband-wife
    (E) All of the above

87. Which of the following characteristics best explains the durability of Confucian ideology in Chinese history?
    I. Its ability to model large-scale relations between groups in the body politic on familial or personal relationships
    II. Its ability to fulfill persistent desires of women for equality in gender relations
    III. Its ability to unify a massive imperial bureaucracy around a common set of moral precepts over time
    IV. A set of widely agreed-on and accepted essential texts, beginning with the Analects, which formed a common basis for study over time
    V. Its exclusively Chinese origin, which meshed well with prevalent notions of the superiority of the "Middle Kingdom" over other civilizations

    (A) I, II, and V
    (B) I, II, and III
    (C) II, III, and IV
    (D) III, IV, and V
    (E) I, III, IV, and V

88. Which of the following choices contains belief systems that originated in China?
    I. Confucianism
    II. Legalism
    III. Daoism
    IV. Buddhism

    (A) I, II, and IV
    (B) I and II
    (C) II and III
    (D) I, II, III, and IV
    (E) I, II, and III

89. Confucianism differed from Hinduism in that

    (A) Confucianism held women as subordinate to men.
    (B) Confucianism detailed the levels of the social hierarchy in more specific terms.
    (C) Confucianism more clearly outlined guidelines for behavior.
    (D) Confucianism was more oriented toward religious devotion and the hereafter.
    (E) Confucianism emphasized earthly obligations without regard to concerns relating to afterlife and rebirth.

90. Which is the closest similarity between the Roman Empire and the Han dynasty of ancient China?

(A) Both aimed for and experienced long periods of isolationism in world affairs.

(B) Both created a government run by elected officials known as Senators.

(C) Both achieved long periods of centralized government and expanding economies.

(D) Both rejected social hierarchy.

(E) Both afforded women equal opportunities to wield political power as men.

91. Which of the following descriptions best summarize the kinds of individuals who have founded a Chinese dynasty?

   I. Military genius of peasant origin
   II. Regional feudal ruler who defeats rivals in battle
   III. Nomadic chieftain
   IV. Confucian scholar-gentry

(A) I, II, and IV

(B) II, III, and IV

(C) I, III, and IV

(D) I, II, and III

(E) I and II

92. One major difference between the fall of Han China and that of the Roman Empire was

(A) Dynastic China would return to equal and even greater prominence.

(B) The Roman Empire left little basis for subsequent developments in Western civilization.

(C) The Roman Empire collapsed due to multiple causes while Han China fell to peasant unrest alone.

(D) Han China adopted a new state religion in its later phase while the Roman Empire did not.

(E) Roman imperial blunders can be traced to decisions made in a Senate, not by emperors.

93. In Chinese tradition, the Mandate of Heaven refers to

(A) Chinese ethnocentric tendencies

(B) Eternal authority of a ruling dynasty

(C) Divine blessing of the rule of an emperor

(D) Belief in many gods

(E) The goal of Buddhist meditation

94. In which of the following periods of Chinese history did Confucius live?

(A) Qin dynasty
(B) Late Zhou dynasty "Era of Warring States"
(C) Han dynasty
(D) Sui dynasty
(E) Shang dynasty

95. Which of the following is true for both the Qin and Han dynasties?

(A) State policy was shaped by Confucian precepts.
(B) Imperial authority was strong in the opening years of each.
(C) Merchants were held in high regard.
(D) Trade was not economically important.
(E) Nomadic invaders toppled each one.

96. Daoist thought tends to emphasize

(A) Respect for the emperor
(B) Harmony with nature
(C) Authority of the father
(D) The struggle of the poor for justice
(E) Punishment for sin

97. Which of the following was NOT a state concern in Han China?

(A) Expanding educational opportunity for elite women
(B) Sponsorship of scientific inquiry
(C) Maintenance of the Great Wall
(D) Grain requisition from the peasantry
(E) Suppression of banditry

98. Daoist conceptions of nature emphasized

(A) A single omnipresent God
(B) Understanding through scientific investigation
(C) Harmony and balance
(D) Numerous minor gods that intervened in human affairs
(E) Presence of fallen human souls in the bodies of animals

99. Daoism was never a threat to dynastic rule because

(A) Daoist doctrine held that the emperor was holiest of all.

(B) Daoists believed the natural order required exploitation of the peasantry.

(C) Daoist religious leaders became the main advisors of the scholar-gentry.

(D) Daoist detachment from human affairs blunted the possibility of political threat.

(E) Daoists abandoned their faith in favor of Confucianism over time.

100. The main pattern in Chinese art established by the close of the classical era was

(A) A focus on monumental building

(B) High levels of craftsmanship and attention to detail work

(C) Reverence of the female physical form

(D) Preference of marble over jade in small sculptures

(E) Representation of the peasantry

CHAPTER 2

The Postclassical Era: 600 CE to 1450

Controlling Idea: Resurgence

The story here is rather simple: as we approach the year 600 we see that the classical civilizations have collapsed, and trade and religion lead the way in the process of recovery. The story of this unit is the story of a regeneration of centralized political authority that first matches and then surpasses levels of imperial cohesion seen in the era of classical civilizations. By 1450 a Resurgence has been completed, and broadly speaking each center of civilization has recovered, consolidated, and expanded upon earlier glories. We also notice that by 1450 the major world religions are established, roughly, in the areas they hold sway until today. The great outlier when speaking in such general terms are the civilizations of the Americas which, while developing along familiar lines seen elsewhere in the Foundations era, are not integrated into global networks of long distance trade by 1450.

101. Which of the following would have been outside the sphere of Mongol control at its height?
   (A) China
   (B) Anatolia
   (C) Persia
   (D) Mesopotamia
   (E) Germany

102. Which long-distance trade network was stabilized in the period historians term the Pax Mongolica (Mongol Peace)?
   (A) Indian Ocean routes
   (B) Triangular trade routes
   (C) East Asian sea routes
   (D) Silk Roads
   (E) Trans-Sahara routes

103. How were individuals selected for leadership in traditional Mongol society?
(A) Hereditary warrior lineage
(B) Long-established aristocratic status
(C) Merit system based on demonstrated battlefield bravery
(D) Divine revelation of chosen ones
(E) Social status based on number of goats, sheep, and horses owned

104. Which of the following does not belong in a list of military tactics or equipment employed by the Mongol armies?
(A) Combination of light and heavy cavalry
(B) Use of the crossbow and short bow
(C) Phalanx infantry formations
(D) Lightweight armor of leather, iron, or silk
(E) Extensive spy network

105. Which of the following was the most decisive change Mongol rule brought to Russia?
(A) Emancipation of the serfs
(B) Migration of the center of power from Kiev to Moscow
(C) Permanent separation of Russian culture from that of the West
(D) Abandonment of the Cyrillic alphabet
(E) Adoption of Buddhism among Russia's elite

106. Which of the following dealt the most devastating blow to the Abbasid caliphate in particular and Islamic civilization in general?
(A) Christian crusader incursions in the Near East
(B) Ottoman Turkic conquest of Constantinople
(C) Mongol invasion of Mesopotamia
(D) U.S. invasions of Iraq and Afghanistan after September 11, 2001
(E) Portuguese defeat of the Ottoman navy

107. Which practices were employed by Kublai Khan and later Yuan dynasty rulers to ensure Mongol dominance in China?
   I.   Refusal to adopt Chinese civil service exams
   II. Dependence on Muslims and nomads, not Confucian bureaucrats, as next in command in the exercise of power
   III. Stubborn clinging to nomadic habits and refusal to settle down and administer the new dynasty from one imperial city

   (A) I and II
   (B) II and III
   (C) I and III
   (D) I, II, and III
   (E) II only

108. Which group benefited from newfound higher status in the period of Mongol rule in China?
   (A) Scholar-gentry
   (B) Aristocracy
   (C) Peasantry
   (D) Merchants
   (E) Buddhist monks

109. Which of the following terms for a political unit does not have the title of its leader as its root word?
   (A) Khanate
   (B) County
   (C) Nation
   (D) Shogunate
   (E) Caliphate

110. Who led a short-lived reemergence of Central Asian nomadic dominance after the fall of the Mongol Empire?
   (A) Suleyman the Magnificent
   (B) Kublai Khan
   (C) Babur
   (D) Timur-I Lang
   (E) Genghis Khan

111. Which military innovation did the Mongols expose Europeans to for the first time?

(A) The catapult
(B) The siege tower
(C) The battle axe
(D) Cavalry units
(E) Gunpowder

112. Which global force was the FIRST to consistently integrate sub-Saharan Africa into a global network of exchange of goods and ideas?

(A) Islamic civilization
(B) Modern globalization
(C) Transatlantic slave trade
(D) The Roman Empire
(E) The conquests of Alexander

113. Which of the following trade networks is limited to the confines of the African continent?

(A) Triangular trade routes
(B) Indian Ocean
(C) East Asian Sea
(D) Trans-Saharan
(E) Silk Roads

114. Which of the following does NOT belong in a list of features of a stateless society?

(A) Delayed ability to respond to external threats
(B) Limited ability to mobilize for war
(C) Mass slave revolt
(D) Difficulty in undertaking large building projects
(E) Lack of stability required for consistent and growing long-distance trade

115. Which of the following was the common unifying feature of sub-Saharan African societies in the postclassical era?

(A) Adoption of Islam by elites
(B) Broad-based expansion of literacy among the masses of the people
(C) Common Bantu linguistic roots
(D) Steam-powered industrial base of the economy
(E) Matriarchal political power

116. As Islam spread, which of the following religious tendencies proved most durable across sub-Saharan Africa?

    (A) Ancestor worship
    (B) Roman Catholicism
    (C) Zen Buddhism
    (D) Coptic Christianity
    (E) Roman polytheism

117. North Africa served as a bridge for Muslim influence to reach which region of the globe?

    (A) Persia
    (B) Central Asia
    (C) Anatolia
    (D) Spain
    (E) Scandinavia

118. Since the classical era, which African region most accurately fits the description "gateway to the Middle East"?

    (A) Ghana
    (B) Zimbabwe
    (C) Egypt
    (D) Congo
    (E) Sudan

119. Which indigenous African ethnic group adopted and vigorously spread Islam?

    (A) Khoisan
    (B) Zulu
    (C) Berber
    (D) Ethiopian
    (E) Bedouin

120. Which African society held on most fiercely to Christianity in the period of Islam's expansion in Africa?

    (A) Egypt and Ethiopia
    (B) Mali
    (C) Ghana
    (D) Songhai
    (E) Tunisia

121. Which does NOT belong in this list of Sudanic states?

(A) Ghana
(B) Mali
(C) Songhai
(D) Congo
(E) Hausa

122. World historians associate the gold-salt trade most closely with which of the following trade routes?

(A) East Asian sea network
(B) Indian Ocean network
(C) Silk Roads
(D) Trans-Saharan routes
(E) Hanseatic League network

123. Which West African leadership figure is best known for his lavish fourteenth-century pilgrimage to Mecca and Medina?

(A) Kwame Nkrumah
(B) Sundiata Keita
(C) Leopold Senghor
(D) Mansa Kankan Musa
(E) Sunni Ali

124. Of the postclassical cities listed below, which was the most sophisticated?

(A) Rome
(B) Timbuktu
(C) Paris
(D) London
(E) Moscow

125. Of the following lists, which places the rise and fall of key West African Sudanic states in proper chronological order?

(A) Mali, Ghana, Songhay
(B) Songhay, Ghana, Mali
(C) Mali, Songhay, Ghana
(D) Ghana, Songhay, Mali
(E) Ghana, Mali, Songhay

126. Which set of practices carried out by devout Muslims in West Africa set their society apart from patterns established in the greater Islamic world?
   (A) Ongoing practice of ancestor worship
   (B) Preference of the spoken over the written word in religious and state affairs
   (C) Fewer restrictions on female dress codes
   (D) Substitution of Timbuktu for Mecca and Medina as a pilgrimage destination
   (E) A tendency to spread Islam through military conquest as opposed to trade

127. Which choice best describes the origins of the Swahili language?
   (A) Bantu-Yoruba mix
   (B) Arabic-Berber mix
   (C) Arabic-Bantu mix
   (D) Yoruba-Arabic mix
   (E) Berber-Bantu mix

128. Which choice best describes the points of origin of goods one might find in a Swahili coast market?
   (A) Chinese, Indian, English
   (B) Islamic, Indian, Chinese
   (C) Scandinavian, Indian, Russian
   (D) Russian, Islamic, English
   (E) English, Chinese, Russian

129. Which of the following does NOT belong in a list of Swahili states of the East African coastline?
   (A) Zanzibar
   (B) Mogadishu
   (C) Timbuktu
   (D) Kilwa
   (E) Mombasa

130. Which of the following materials is most associated with premodern sub-Saharan African artistic expertise?
   (A) Marble
   (B) Oil paints
   (C) Mosaic tile
   (D) Ivory
   (E) Jade

131. Which of the following is NOT one of the ways Islam helped strengthen the authority of ruling elites as it spread across the African continent?

(A) Introduction of the written word, which streamlined political administration

(B) Conversion of a majority of commoners, creating a new basis for unity across all classes

(C) Ability to access goods from distant lands through Islamic trade networks

(D) Absorption of techniques of rule from wider Islamic civilization

(E) Ability to facilitate access to distant markets where African raw materials were in demand

132. Which of the following does NOT belong in a list of similarities in the process of how Islam spread to South Asia, Southeast Asia, and Africa?

(A) Islam arrived with traders and took root first in urban areas.

(B) The spread of Islam was mainly peaceful.

(C) Political power remained in the hands of non-Arab elites.

(D) Considerable syncretism was involved in the conversion process.

(E) A majority of the population in all three areas converted to Islam.

133. Which religious schism stemmed from disputes over legitimate succession of leadership after the death of its key or founding figure?

(A) Eastern Orthodox and Catholic

(B) Catholic and Protestant

(C) Mahayana and Theravada

(D) Sunni and Shia

(E) Mahayana and Zen

134. Which best qualifies as the largest durable tricontinental civilization?

(A) Roman

(B) Hellenistic

(C) Islamic

(D) Han

(E) Mongol

135. Pre-Islamic Arab society is best characterized as

(A) Pastoral nomadic

(B) Sedentary agricultural

(C) Highly urbanized

(D) Maritime trade-based

(E) Hunter-gatherer

136. Which two Muslim cities retain the greatest symbolic or religious significance in Islam to this day?
   I. Baghdad
   II. Istanbul
   III. Mecca
   IV. Timbuktu
   V. Medina

   (A) I and II
   (B) II and III
   (C) II and IV
   (D) III and V
   (E) IV and V

137. Which two Muslim cities served as political and administrative centers of Muslim empires?
   I. Baghdad
   II. Istanbul
   III. Mecca
   IV. Mogadishu
   V. Medina

   (A) I and III
   (B) II and IV
   (C) I and II
   (D) III and V
   (E) II and V

138. Upon whom did Muhammad depend most directly for economic support?
   (A) Local chieftains
   (B) The urban poor
   (C) His wife, Khadija
   (D) Roman imperial administrators
   (E) Byzantine merchants

139. Which of the following Arabic terms refers to the "community of the faithful"?
   (A) Hijab
   (B) Hajj
   (C) Hadith
   (D) Zakat
   (E) Umma

140. Which neighboring empires faced the challenge of Umayyad expansion?
    I. Roman
    II. Gupta
   III. Sassanid Persia
   IV. Byzantine
    V. Han

(A) I and II
(B) II and IV
(C) III and V
(D) III and IV
(E) II and V

141. Which choice best describes the eastern and western geographic limits of Islamic rule at its greatest extent during the period of the Umayyad and Abbasid caliphates?

(A) Northwest India to Spain and Morocco
(B) Eastern Mediterranean to Persia
(C) Arabian peninsula to the Tigris-Euphrates Valley
(D) Persia to Southeast Asia
(E) East Asia to Spain and Morocco

142. Who would not have qualified as part of the group labeled the "dhimmi" in the Abbasid caliphate?

(A) Jews
(B) Catholics
(C) Greek Orthodox
(D) Animist
(E) Hindu

143. Which choice does NOT belong in a list describing the status of Muslim women in the early Islamic period?

(A) Male adultery was condemned in the Koran.
(B) Female infanticide was forbidden.
(C) Females and males both were allowed multiple spouses.
(D) Female inheritance rights were strengthened.
(E) Divorce rights for women existed.

144. In which postclassical civilization did women enjoy the highest status?
- (A) Tang China
- (B) Islamic
- (C) Byzantine
- (D) Carolingian
- (E) Heian Japan

145. Which Muslim group overthrew the Umayyad dynasty and set up a new caliphate?
- (A) Sassanids
- (B) Seljuks
- (C) Abbasids
- (D) Swahilis
- (E) Sunnis

146. Which city became the capital of the Abbasid Empire and a center of what has been termed an Islamic golden age?
- (A) Istanbul
- (B) Timbuktu
- (C) Seville
- (D) Baghdad
- (E) Samarkand

147. Which of the following areas of expertise or learning progressed under the rule of the Abbasid caliphate?
- (A) Medicine
- (B) Law
- (C) Philosophy
- (D) Mathematics
- (E) All of the above

148. Which of the following does NOT belong in a list of characteristics common to the decline of both the Roman and Abbasid empires?
- (A) Chaotic succession fights for the imperial throne
- (B) Frequent interference of military commanders in politics
- (C) Growing dependence on nomadic warriors or mercenaries
- (D) Decline in agricultural productivity
- (E) Imperial conversion to a new religion

149. What is the name of the peninsula that served as the homeland of the Byzantine and, later, the Ottoman Empire?

(A) Anatolia
(B) Horn of Africa
(C) Iberian
(D) Florida
(E) Italian

150. What was the main global impact of the Crusades?

I. Western Europeans gained permanent bases in the Middle East.
II. Islam split into the Sunni and Shia branches.
III. Western Europeans were reintroduced to the knowledge and trade of a more civilized world.
IV. Christianity became the dominant religion in Jerusalem.

(A) I, II, and III
(B) I, II, and IV
(C) III and IV
(D) I only
(E) IV only

151. The proliferation of technical advances and growing wealth of cities in the Abbasid Middle East was most closely matched by which contemporaneous area of civilization?

(A) Mississippian North America
(B) Song China
(C) Great Zimbabwe
(D) Western Europe
(E) Russia

152. Which region, while under Muslim control, remained the least converted and integrated into the global civilization constructed in the era of the Umayyad and Abbasid caliphates?

(A) South Asia
(B) East Asia
(C) Anatolian Peninsula
(D) Egypt
(E) Morocco

153. Which intellectual or technological advancement CANNOT be traced to the era when Islamic civilization was at its height?

(A) Lateen sails
(B) Adoption of Arabic numerals
(C) Anatomical knowledge
(D) Steam-powered industry
(E) Philosophical inquiry

154. Which of the following European regions felt the influence of Byzantine civilization in the postclassical era?

(A) Russia
(B) The Balkans
(C) Ukraine
(D) Belarus
(E) All of the above

155. After the fall of the western portion of the Roman Empire, the official tongue in Constantinople shifted from Latin to which of the following?

(A) Turkish
(B) Persian
(C) Chinese
(D) Arabic
(E) Greek

156. The Byzantine Empire flourished as a crossroads of trade from which regions?

(A) Mediterranean, the Middle East, and Asia
(B) India, Mediterranean, and Asia
(C) Sub-Saharan Africa, India, and the Middle East
(D) The Middle East, Asia, and Scandinavia
(E) Scandinavia, Mediterranean, and India

157. Which early Byzantine emperor had the longest lasting impact on civilization in the eastern Mediterranean and beyond?

(A) Diocletian
(B) Constantine
(C) Justinian
(D) Osman
(E) Muhammad

158. Which of the following does NOT belong in a list of similarities between Byzantine and dynastic Chinese political rule in the Tang era?

(A) An imperial bureaucracy staffed by persons from all social classes but generally drawn from the aristocracy
(B) A throne occasionally held by women
(C) An emperor whose rule has God's approval
(D) Regional governors appointed by the imperial center
(E) Focused initiative to expand territorial boundaries of the empire

159. Russian civilization emerged nearest to what modern-day city?

(A) St. Petersburg
(B) Kiev
(C) Moscow
(D) Warsaw
(E) Paris

160. Kievan Rus is unique in world history because

(A) It mediated contact between the Byzantine Empire and more distant lands.
(B) It is the birthplace of Islam.
(C) It was, in land area, the largest single European state of the postclassical era.
(D) It adopted religious and bureaucratic practices from a neighboring civilization.
(E) It toppled the Roman Empire.

161. Which ideology gained influence in the period of disorder that followed the collapse of the Han dynasty?

(A) Confucianism
(B) Buddhism
(C) Daoism
(D) Mao Zedong Thought
(E) Legalism

162. Which dynasty built the largest land empire?

(A) Zhou
(B) Han
(C) Tang
(D) Song
(E) Ming

163. Which is most true about the staffing of the central administration of the imperial bureaucracy in the Tang-Song era?
    (A) Gifted females were targeted for rapid promotion.
    (B) Positions were dominated by sinicized nomads.
    (C) Administrators were selected by the emperor.
    (D) The staff comprised individuals from prominent families.
    (E) Administrators were selected based on most effective tax collection techniques.

164. Which of the following statements best describes the status of the Buddhist faith in China after the persecutions of the Tang era?
    (A) Chinese emperors continued to practice Buddhism.
    (B) Buddhism grew rapidly as a form of rebellion against a hated imperial bureaucracy.
    (C) Buddhism disappeared completely from Chinese society.
    (D) Presence of Buddhist monasteries and practice remained relatively unchanged.
    (E) Buddhism continued to exist, but on a much reduced scale.

165. Neo-Confucianism incorporated ideas from which of the following belief systems that had grown in popularity in China?
    I. Hinduism
    II. Buddhism
    III. Daoism
    IV. Islam
    (A) I and II
    (B) II and III
    (C) III and IV
    (D) I, II, and III
    (E) II, III, and IV

166. Which of the following is NOT a nomadic group that pressured dynastic rule at some point over the course of Chinese history?
    (A) Jurchen
    (B) Mongol
    (C) Turk
    (D) Manchu
    (E) Tibetan

167. Which do historians point to as the key infrastructural development of the Tang-Song era?

(A) Construction of the Great Wall
(B) Construction of a national highway system
(C) Construction of the Forbidden City
(D) Construction of the Grand Canal
(E) Construction of the port at Canton

168. Which practice dates from the Song era?

(A) Foot binding
(B) Arranged marriage
(C) Concubinage
(D) Divorce rights
(E) One-child policy

169. Which is not a native Chinese invention?

(A) Explosive powder
(B) Magnetic compass
(C) Movable type
(D) Paper money
(E) Steam-powered machinery

170. What is the title earned by students who passed the most difficult battery of Chinese civil service examinations?

(A) Gentry
(B) Ninja
(C) Sensei
(D) Jinshi
(E) Eunuch

171. Which is NOT an effect of the emergence of neo-Confucianism in the Tang-Song era?

(A) Regeneration of a centralized bureaucracy
(B) Preference of Chinese ideas and practices over foreign ones
(C) Growing egalitarianism in gender roles
(D) Development of public works
(E) Institution of a more rigorous education and examination system

172. Despite extensive modeling of the Chinese imperial system, how did Japanese civilization hew to established tradition in the postclassical era?

    (A) Aristocrats doubled as military officers.

    (B) Strict codes of behavior governed noble classes in court life at the imperial center.

    (C) Examination systems were not a part of the selection process for the imperial elite.

    (D) Poetry was a highly valued art form among the elite.

    (E) A capital city served as the nerve center of the empire.

173. Which of the following peoples would have been outside of the Chinese tribute system in East Asia in the Tang-Song era?

    (A) Korean

    (B) Vietnamese

    (C) Japanese

    (D) Polynesian

    (E) Tibetan

174. Where in the world did the literary form of the novel emerge?

    (A) United States

    (B) Japan

    (C) France

    (D) England

    (E) India

175. Which contemporary society most closely mirrored feudal Japanese patterns of decentralized rule, an economy based on agricultural peasant labor, and emergence of a warrior elite following a distinct code of honor?

    (A) Polynesian

    (B) Inca

    (C) Western European

    (D) Russian

    (E) Islamic

176. Which of the following do historians most closely associate with the period of Western history known as the High Middle Ages?

(A) Carolingian France

(B) Steam-powered Industrial Revolution

(C) Enclosure movement and the rise of commercial agriculture

(D) Gothic architecture, the Crusades, and the rise of the Western university

(E) Frequent Viking incursions and raids along European coastlines and rivers

177. Which of the following regions of Western Europe remained most insulated from the general trend toward disorder following the fall of the Roman Empire?

(A) France

(B) England

(C) Germany

(D) Spain

(E) Italy

178. Which group was most likely to be literate in the period of European history often called the Dark Ages?

(A) Aristocrats

(B) Peasants

(C) Monks

(D) Knights

(E) Monarchs

179. Which of the following terms matches this definition: "agricultural laborer tied to an estate with rights including military protection, heritable ownership of a plot of land, and owing obligations to share crop yields each season with his or her lord."

(A) Peasant

(B) Slave

(C) Proletarian

(D) Serf

(E) Plebian

180. Which of the following possessed the greatest unified organizational capacity across the largest land area in Western Europe in the centuries immediately following the fall of the Roman Empire?

(A) Holy Roman Empire
(B) Islamic caliphates
(C) Catholic church
(D) Carolingian monarchy
(E) Mongol Empire

181. Which best characterizes the impact of the Magna Carta?

(A) The principle of limited monarchy and representative bodies was established.
(B) More accurate maps were produced.
(C) Universal manhood suffrage became the norm in feudal societies.
(D) Parliamentary rule replaced monarchy across the West.
(E) Increasingly, females came to wield political power.

182. Which of the following does NOT belong in a list of territorial expansionary moves by Western powers in the postclassical era?

(A) Germanic settlement in Poland
(B) Iberian offensives against Islamic presence in Spain
(C) Crusades to the Middle East
(D) Viking voyages across the North Atlantic
(E) Belgian penetration of the Congo

183. Which term do historians associate with medieval Western inquiry that sought to reconcile reason and religious faith and is most closely associated with the thinking of St. Thomas Aquinas?

(A) Confucianism
(B) Existentialism
(C) Scholasticism
(D) Eclecticism
(E) Marxism

184. Which body of water was the scene of trade involving merchant ships from the most diverse collection of civilizations in the postclassical era?

(A) Atlantic Ocean
(B) Pacific Ocean
(C) Baltic Sea
(D) Indian Ocean
(E) Caribbean Sea

185. Which of the following does not belong in this list of Western postclassical literary works written in vernacular tongues?

(A) *The Song of Roland*, unknown author
(B) *The Canterbury Tales*, Geoffrey Chaucer
(C) *The Decameron*, Giovanni Bocccio
(D) *Beowulf*, unknown
(E) *Summa Theologica*, St. Thomas Aquinas

186. Which of the following organizations grouped town dwellers by occupation, regulated apprenticeships, and upheld standards of workmanship?

(A) Parliaments
(B) Estates General
(C) Guilds
(D) Communes
(E) Monasteries

187. By which route would medieval women have been most likely to find an alternative path in life outside of marriage?

(A) Practicing witchcraft
(B) Joining a crusade
(C) Becoming a nun
(D) Entering banking
(E) Joining the priesthood

188. What is the name of the conflict that consumed England and France in the late postclassical era?

(A) Seven Years' War
(B) World War I
(C) Hundred Years' War
(D) Thirty Years' War
(E) World War II

189. Of those listed below, which civilization existed in the most complete state of isolation in the period 600–1450?

(A) Ming China
(B) Delhi Sultanate
(C) Aztec Empire
(D) Carolingian France
(E) Kievan Rus

190. Which of the following best characterizes similarities between Aztec and Inca civilizations?
  I. Grew out of long development of preceding civilizations
  II. Nobility formed the personnel of the state
  III. Climatic and topographical setting

(A) I and II
(B) II and III
(C) I and III
(D) II only
(E) III only

191. Maya, Aztec, and Inca civilization managed to construct monumental structures without which of the following?

(A) Writing systems
(B) State authority
(C) Draft animals
(D) Slave labor
(E) Stone tools

192. Along with Venice in Italy, what other postclassical city is famous for its dependence on boats and canals as the primary means of urban transport?

(A) Chang'an
(B) Tenochtitlan
(C) London
(D) Samarkand
(E) Timbuktu

193. All of the following statements concerning Aztec human sacrifice are accurate EXCEPT

(A) It was a preexisting religious ritual as the Aztecs rose to power.
(B) It became more frequent under Aztec rule.
(C) It was accompanied at times by ritual cannibalism.
(D) It was pointed to by conquistadores and others to justify Spanish colonization.
(E) Members of the Aztec ruling elite constituted the bulk of the individuals sacrificed.

194. Which class played a central role in the Aztec economy and was more highly respected there than in contemporary China?

(A) Warrior
(B) Peasant
(C) Aristocracy
(D) Merchant
(E) Artisan

195. What is the name of the family units into which Aztec society was organized and accounted for by the state bureaucracy?

(A) Ayllu
(B) Maize
(C) Calpulli
(D) Clans
(E) Tribes

196. The regard with which the Inca held their monarch is analogous to which concepts we see in postclassical and early modern "Old World" civilizations?

  I. Constitutional monarchy
 II. The Mandate of Heaven
III. The "divine right" of kings

(A) I and II
(B) II and III
(C) I and III
(D) I only
(E) II only

197. Which classical civilizations were most famous for their extensive and centrally planned imperial road networks?

  I. Roman Empire
 II. Aztec Empire
III. Inca Empire
IV. Mongol Empire

(A) I and II
(B) II and III
(C) I and IV
(D) I and III
(E) II and IV

198. Which Inca city remains an important urban center in Peru today?

(A) Tenochtitlan
(B) Machu Picchu
(C) New Orleans
(D) Bogota
(E) Cuzco

199. Which of the following best describes the region where the Inca civilization flourished?

(A) Andean highland and Pacific coast
(B) Amazon basin and Valley of Mexico
(C) Mississippi river basin and Andean highlands
(D) Valley of Mexico and Andean highlands
(E) Pacific coast and Valley of Mexico

200. Which was the most densely populated region of the Americas by the end of the postclassical era?

(A) Eastern woodlands region of North America
(B) Pacific northwest region of North America
(C) Southern cone of South America
(D) Amazon river basin of South America
(E) Valley of Mexico in Mesoamerica

CHAPTER 3

The Early Modern Era: 1450 to 1750

Controlling Idea: The First Global Age

In this unit the big news, so to speak, is that the North and South American continents are integrated into global long distance trade networks for the first time. While all civilizations are in ever closer contact it is the West that works its way to the center of the world trading network, serving as intermediaries in the ever greater volumes of trade that wash across the globe between 1450 and 1750. While not dominant by 1750 (except over the Americas) the West nonetheless is becoming positioned to capitalize off its emergent role at the "core" of a new world economy, and the slow integration of the world into a single economic unit begins in this period and has accelerated down to today.

201. Which of the following does NOT belong in a list of factors preventing European powers from establishing anything more than a limited coastal settlement on the African continent in the period 1450–1750?

   (A) Climate
   (B) Disease
   (C) Impassable rivers
   (D) Stiff organized African resistance
   (E) Inferior weapons technology

202. Which European power was first to establish large-scale slave-trading operations on the African continent for the purposes of export to plantations in the Americas?

   (A) Spain
   (B) England
   (C) Portugal
   (D) France
   (E) Netherlands

203. In which century did the Atlantic slave trade peak in terms of numbers of Africans transported?
(A) Fifteenth
(B) Sixteenth
(C) Seventeenth
(D) Eighteenth
(E) Nineteenth

204. Which trend was most typical in slave-capturing coastal West African kingdoms, such as Dahomey, which supplied the Atlantic slave trade?
(A) Mass conversion to Christianity
(B) Increasing hierarchy, centralization, and importance of military capacity including use of firearms
(C) Depopulation as younger generations were shipped away
(D) Industrialization as a result of capital accumulation due to slave trade
(E) Development of representative democracy

205. Which would be the LEAST typical trade transaction along Africa's northeast coast in the period 1450–1750?
(A) Ivory exported to India
(B) Gold exported to Persia
(C) Female slaves exported to Arabian peninsula for domestic labor
(D) Female slaves exported to a West Indies sugar plantation
(E) Copies of the Koran imported to coastal towns

206. The Afrikaners who settled in southern Africa traced their origin back to which European region?
(A) England
(B) Germany
(C) Netherlands
(D) France
(E) Spain

207. What is the best way to characterize relations between the British and the Afrikaners after the British arrived in southern Africa in 1795?
(A) Hostility and complete social segregation
(B) Maintenance of Afrikaner political supremacy
(C) Britain gains formal possession of the colony, but conflict persists with Afrikaners over land and expansion
(D) Complete unity in the face of superior African military strength
(E) Negotiated division of southern Africa into British and Afrikaner spheres of roughly equal size and importance

208. Which is most true of the Middle Passage?

(A) It was generally a pleasant voyage.
(B) Mortality on marches to the African coast was higher than mortality on the ships.
(C) It generally lasted a year or more.
(D) African naval expertise was key to guiding vessels across the Atlantic.
(E) It was not driven by the profit motive.

209. In which New World society did the slave population grow mainly through natural increase and not continued importation?

(A) Haiti
(B) Jamaica
(C) Argentina
(D) Southern British North American colonies
(E) Barbados

210. Where in the New World did slavery last the longest?

(A) Haiti
(B) Brazil
(C) Cuba
(D) The United States
(E) Mexico

211. To which location was the greatest number of enslaved Africans transported?

(A) Spanish Mexico
(B) Portuguese Brazil
(C) British North America
(D) Dutch Indonesia
(E) French Saint-Domingue (Haiti)

212. Which Western power was first to ban its citizens from engaging in the slave trade?

(A) France
(B) England
(C) United States
(D) Portugal
(E) Spain

213. Which Western tradition did the continuation of the Atlantic slave trade violate most?

(A) Enlightenment
(B) Greco-Roman
(C) Feudal
(D) Mercantilist
(E) Absolutist

214. Which monarchy constructed the largest contiguous land empire in history, second in size only to the Mongol Empire?

(A) British
(B) Mughal
(C) Russian
(D) French
(E) Qing

215. In which neighboring region(s) did the Russian Empire gain the most land during the Romanov dynasty?

(A) Poland
(B) Baltic States
(C) Black Sea region
(D) Siberia and Central Asia
(E) Scandinavia

216. The shift of the Russian imperial capital to which city indicated a shift in orientation toward the West under the rule of Peter the Great?

(A) Moscow
(B) Kiev
(C) Vladivostok
(D) St. Petersburg
(E) Belgrade

217. Which of the following was unique to Russian industrial development in the czarist period?

(A) Use of serf labor in factories
(B) Application of heavy industry to military uses
(C) Growing urbanization
(D) Increased importance of the mining sector of the economy
(E) Tremendous opportunities for profit making

218. Which of the following best describes the attitude of Peter and Catherine the Great toward adopting change along Western lines?

(A) It was a waste of time and an insult to Russian tradition.

(B) Its harmless influence was allowed to spread without interference.

(C) It was a source of new ideas and methods to increase the power of the ruling family at home and abroad.

(D) It was a key step on the road to Russian democracy.

(E) Emulation of Western gender roles but not economic practices would be pursued.

219. Which Russian territorial possession lay farthest from the center of power in St. Petersburg?

(A) Alaska

(B) Finland

(C) Crimea

(D) Siberia

(E) Poland

220. How did Russia tend to fit into the emerging global economy in the period 1450–1750?

(A) As a source of serf labor transported to till the soils of Western Europe

(B) As a market for grain grown in the New World

(C) As the primary Old World destination of the silver being taken out of the New World

(D) As a supplier of grain, timber, fur, and other raw materials to the West

(E) As a center of industrial development based on export of finished goods

221. Which feature of the expanding Russian Empire in the period 1500–1800 was NOT a feature of expanding Western European empires in this period?

(A) Russia held military dominance over less technologically sophisticated peoples.

(B) Multiple ethnicities fell under the rule of a single monarch.

(C) Territorial expansion was a major goal.

(D) Natural resources and agricultural products were extracted from the newly absorbed lands.

(E) Expansion was mainly carried out over land and not sea.

222. Which end result of industrial development was most important to Peter the Great?

(A) Russian capacity to produce modern weapons
(B) Growth of a vibrant merchant class
(C) A raised cultural level of the resultant urban masses
(D) Ability to project naval power across the Pacific Ocean
(E) More ideal conditions for the growth of the Bolshevik party

223. Which impulse for the colonization of North America was generally missing from the colonization of the rest of the New World?

(A) Setting up slave plantations
(B) The search for gold
(C) Freedom from religious persecution
(D) Expansion of royal authority
(E) Missionary drive to convert Native Americans to Christianity

224. The economic centrality of long-distance trade and the lack of long feudal traditions opened a path for which social class to rise to dominance relatively quickly in the New World?

(A) Independent farmer/peasant
(B) Proletarian
(C) Merchant
(D) Aristocracy
(E) Monarchy

225. How was racial hierarchy on the North American continent different from racial hierarchy in Spanish Latin America?

(A) Intermarriage among Native American, African, and European populations was much less common.
(B) Enslaved Africans could as a rule look forward to manumission upon the death of his or her owner.
(C) Native Americans were preferred over Africans to perform slave labor.
(D) European settlers formed a smaller minority of the overall population.
(E) Native American leaders enjoyed equal political and social status as European elites in colonial society.

226. In which colonized region of the globe did Western cultural practices supplant existing cultural practices most completely after 1450?

(A) West Africa

(B) North and South America

(C) East Asia

(D) South Asia

(E) South Africa

227. In which way did the Spanish colonies reproduce existing Iberian social structures?

(A) Colonies were established as monarchies in their own right.

(B) Gender roles were preserved from the very start as equal proportions of Spanish males and females settled the New World.

(C) Peninsulares sought to reproduce essentially feudal estates with indigenous labor filling the role of the Spanish serf.

(D) Religious toleration remained an important factor in integrating diverse peoples into a cohesive social unit.

(E) Extended families continued to live in clan compounds headed by matriarchal authority figures.

228. Which region of the New World saw the initial penetration by European explorers and subjugation of the Native population to slave labor?

(A) Mesoamerica

(B) Andean South America

(C) Caribbean Islands

(D) Atlantic shoreline of North America

(E) Atlantic shoreline of South America

229. Which of the following accompanied the transition from conquest to settlement of the New World?

(A) Transition from the search for gold to setting up of ranches and sugar plantations

(B) Increased emigration of Spanish women to the New World

(C) Disappearance of the majority of the indigenous population through disease or killing

(D) Importation of African slaves to work plantations

(E) All of the above

230. Which New World commodity was of the greatest value to the Spanish monarchy?

    (A) Potato

    (B) Tomato

    (C) Silver

    (D) Sugar

    (E) Quinine

231. What was the long-term impact of the massive influx of silver into the Spanish economy that resulted from its domination of the New World?

    I. Inflation and unwise government spending

    II. A permanent economic advantage over other European powers

    III. Development of the most sophisticated banking system in the world

    (A) I only

    (B) II only

    (C) III only

    (D) I and II

    (E) I and III

232. Which New World commodity was of the greatest value to the Portuguese monarchy in the early phases of the settlement of Brazil?

    (A) Potato

    (B) Tomato

    (C) Silver

    (D) Sugar

    (E) Quinine

233. Which of the following choices places Latin America's racial hierarchy in the proper order, from lowest to highest, in status?

    (A) Mestizo/mulatto, Native American/African slave, Peninsular, Creole

    (B) Native American/African slave, mestizo/mulatto, Creole, Peninsular

    (C) Peninsular, Creole, mestizo/mulatto, Native American/African slave

    (D) Creole, mestizo/mulatto, Peninsular, Native American/African slave

    (E) Native American/African slave, Creole, mestizo/mulatto, Peninsular

234. Which statement best characterizes the political situation in the West around 1450?

(A) Highly centralized and powerful monarchies governed linguistically homogeneous kingdoms.

(B) Renaissance ideas had spread, making democracy the preferred political system.

(C) Small political units led by local and regional aristocrats were the rule, not the exception.

(D) The nation-state had taken root and monarchy had passed from the scene.

(E) The Holy Roman Empire had united the West into a larger political unit than the Roman Empire of the classical era.

235. Which label best characterizes the Italian Renaissance?

(A) A political movement

(B) A cultural movement

(C) A religious movement

(D) A mass movement

(E) A global movement

236. Why did the Renaissance originate in the city-states of northern Italy?

(A) Urban artisans provided financial backing.

(B) Expatriate Chinese artists settled there, provided artistic training.

(C) Urban elites grown rich in trade hubs provided financial backing.

(D) The bubonic plague depopulated the countryside more heavily, destroying rural centers of artistic innovation.

(E) Techniques left behind after Ottoman occupation formed the basis for new explorations in art.

237. Which of the following were targeted in the Spanish "Reconquista" of the late fifteenth century?

(A) Muslims and Huguenots

(B) Huguenots and Jews

(C) Catholics and Jews

(D) Muslims and Jews

(E) Catholics and Huguenots

238. Which event is most closely associated with the "reintroduction" of the West to the knowledge and trade of the Middle and Far East after the year 1000?

(A) The voyages of Vasco da Gama
(B) The Black Death
(C) The travels of Ibn Battuta
(D) The Crusades
(E) The travels of Marco Polo

239. Which modern-day European nation projects farthest west off the Eurasian landmass and into the Atlantic Ocean?

(A) Germany
(B) France
(C) England
(D) Portugal
(E) Netherlands

240. Which European naval power is generally credited with breaking the grip on Atlantic maritime trade previously held by the Spanish monarchy?

(A) Holland
(B) Denmark
(C) England
(D) Germany
(E) Norway

241. Which of the following does NOT belong in a list of Catholic doctrines rejected by Martin Luther?

(A) Papal authority
(B) Granting of indulgences
(C) Monasticism
(D) Priestly celibacy
(E) Acceptance of the Holy Trinity

242. Where did Luther's movement first take root?

(A) France
(B) England
(C) Spain
(D) Italy
(E) Germany

243. Which group traces its roots to the Catholic Reformation, sometimes referred to as the Counter-Reformation?

(A) Benedictine monks
(B) Coptic Christians
(C) Jesuits
(D) Liberation theologians
(E) Calvinists

244. Which social class experienced the most growth in absolute numbers as a result of the commercialization of the Western economy in the period 1450–1750?

(A) Peasantry
(B) Proletarians
(C) Merchants
(D) Aristocracy
(E) Clergy

245. Which movement from the following list established a tradition of seeking answers to questions about nature through the application of reason and methodical investigation of the world?

(A) Phenomenology
(B) Scientific Revolution
(C) Protestant Reformation
(D) Enlightenment
(E) Renaissance

246. Which of the following movements applied reason to the problems of human affairs and can be understood as an extension of the Scientific Revolution into the field of politics?

(A) Renaissance
(B) Green Revolution
(C) Enlightenment
(D) Protestant Reformation
(E) Bolshevik Revolution

247. Who is credited with bringing awareness of the heliocentric nature of the solar system into Western civilization?

(A) Aristotle
(B) Galileo
(C) Columbus
(D) Copernicus
(E) Descartes

248. Which of the following thinkers established the principles of objects in motion and defined the forces of gravity?

(A) Descartes
(B) Rousseau
(C) Newton
(D) Bacon
(E) Galileo

249. The following ideas from the Declaration of Independence can be attributed most directly to the influence of whom?

We hold these truths to be *self-evident,* that *all men are created equal,* that they are endowed by their *Creator* with certain *unalienable Rights, [71]* that among these are *Life, Liberty and the pursuit of Happiness.* That to secure these rights, Governments are instituted among Men, deriving their just powers from the *consent of the governed,* That whenever any Form of Government becomes destructive of these ends, it is the *Right of the People to alter or to abolish it,* and to institute new Government, laying its foundation on such principles and organizing its powers in such form, as to them shall seem most likely to effect their Safety and Happiness.

(A) John Locke
(B) Rene Descartes
(C) Michel de Montaigne
(D) Alexis de Toqueville
(E) George Washington

250. Compared, broadly speaking, with other centers of civilization in the world, which of the following had become the most distinctive characteristic of Western intellectual life by about 1750?

(A) Concern with manipulation of nature to serve human interests
(B) Centrality of science in understanding reality
(C) Appreciation of poetry in elite circles
(D) Importance of the written word in preservation of the wisdom of the past
(E) Innovation resulting from exposure to the knowledge and practices of other civilizations

251. Which group suffered the greatest loss of authority as absolute monarchy took hold in the West beginning in the seventeenth century?

(A) Monarchs
(B) Merchants
(C) Peasants
(D) Aristocrats
(E) Artisans

252. Which of the following kingdoms serves as an exception to the rule of the growing power of absolute monarchies in the West in the period 1450–1750?

(A) Spain
(B) France
(C) Austria-Hungary
(D) Prussia
(E) England

253. Which event established the basic sovereignty of Parliament over the king of England?

(A) Reform Act of 1832
(B) The Corn Laws
(C) The Magna Carta
(D) The Glorious Revolution
(E) The American Revolution

254. The relationship between supply and demand, as well as the concepts of "laissez-faire" and the "invisible hand of the market," can be traced to the writings of

(A) Karl Marx
(B) David Ricardo
(C) Adam Smith
(D) Napoleon Bonaparte
(E) Giovanni Boccaccio

255. Which of the following does NOT belong in a list of principles we can identify with the intellectual movement known as the Enlightenment?

(A) Reason is the way to truth.
(B) Rulers are blessed by the divine.
(C) Humans are naturally good.
(D) Blind faith in religion is wrong.
(E) People have rights.

256. Which of the following is another way to express the immediate precursor to the factory system of production that arose in England that is sometimes termed protoindustrialization?

(A) Specialization of labor
(B) Mass assembly line production
(C) The three-field system
(D) Cottage industry
(E) Guild production

257. The factories of the Industrial Revolution depended most heavily on the labor of which of the following groups?

(A) Landed peasantry
(B) Aristocracy
(C) Proletarians
(D) Merchants
(E) Master craftsmen

258. Which of the following branches of Protestantism can trace its roots to a royal figure?

(A) Presbyterian
(B) Calvinism
(C) Lutheranism
(D) Anabaptist
(E) Anglican

259. Which of the following effects best captures the impact of the Mongol Empire on world history?
    I. Spread of the bubonic plague across the Eurasian landmass
    II. Stabilization of long-distance trade routes, which sparked greater demand for goods from distant lands
    III. The exposure of old centers of civilization to new religious and intellectual trends

    (A) I and II
    (B) II and III
    (C) I and III
    (D) I, II, and III
    (E) II only

260. Which statement best characterizes power relations among the centers of Eurasian civilizations as they approached the year 1450?
    (A) Islamic caliphates are reaching the height of their power and influence.
    (B) Ming rulers of China have redoubled their efforts to move to the center of maritime trading networks in the East Asian and Indian Ocean.
    (C) A power vacuum of sorts has opened, as Byzantine, Abbasid, and Ming Chinese powers become less of a force in global affairs.
    (D) Western Europe dominates world trade.
    (E) South and East Asia are no longer important sources of luxury items in long-distance trade networks and become increasingly isolated.

261. How do historians explain the Ming dynasty's 1433 decision to abandon the treasure ship voyages to the Indian Ocean basin that could have placed China at the core of the developing world economy?
    (A) State resources were required to thwart nomadic incursions from beyond the Great Wall.
    (B) A dominant neo-Confucian worldview de-emphasized the value of non-Chinese ideas and products.
    (C) State-backed exploration of distant lands was an unusual experiment in Chinese history.
    (D) Internal economic development was flourishing, making long-distance trade unnecessary.
    (E) All of the above

262. Which of the following were the first slave-based island plantation colonies set up by Western powers?

(A) Bahamas
(B) Ireland
(C) Canary and Madeiras Islands
(D) Hispanola
(E) Jamaica

263. Which of the following can be characterized as outside the world network of trade in 1450?

(A) Ireland
(B) Scandinavia
(C) East Africa
(D) Mesoamerica
(E) The Philippines

264. We associate the Maori people with which of the following locations?

(A) Tasmania
(B) Azores
(C) New Zealand
(D) Hawaii
(E) Polynesia

265. Which of the following established a line of demarcation separating Spanish and Portuguese claims in the New World?

(A) Treaty of Versailles
(B) Edict of Nantes
(C) Treaty of Westphalia
(D) Treaty of Tordesillas
(E) Luther's 95 Theses

266. Which European power won the colony of Indonesia away from the Portuguese in the seventeenth century?

(A) England
(B) Spain
(C) France
(D) Holland
(E) Italy

267. Which colony was claimed by Spain as a result of Ferdinand Magellan's circumnavigation of the globe in 1519–1521?

(A) Madagascar
(B) Hispanola
(C) Mexico
(D) The Philippines
(E) Canary Islands

268. Which event outside the West contributed to creating an opening for the West to move to the core of a global maritime trade network?

(A) Ming reversal of treasure ship voyages in 1433
(B) Fall of the Byzantine Empire after the Ottoman sacking of Constantinople in 1453
(C) Mongol destruction of Abbasid power in 1253
(D) Collapse of Mongol power in the mid-fifteenth century
(E) All of the above

269. Which is an example of a new disease Europeans were exposed to as a result of interaction with the peoples of the New World?

(A) Measles
(B) Mumps
(C) Smallpox
(D) Acquired immunodeficiency syndrome (AIDS)
(E) Syphilis

270. What was the demographic impact of the Columbian Exchange on the populations of the Old World?

(A) Population growth across the Old World based on New World crops such as corn and the potato
(B) Massive depopulation of Western Europe due to migration to the Americas
(C) Sharp increase in the West African population to furnish individuals for the slave trade
(D) Sharp decrease in male populations as many sailors died at sea
(E) Greatly increased life expectancy aided by new medicinal plants from New World tropical rainforests

271. In which regional waterways did the West most rapidly emerge into a dominant position after 1450?

(A) Eastern Mediterranean
(B) South China Sea
(C) Arabian Sea
(D) Caribbean Sea
(E) Yellow Sea

272. What common characteristic can be ascribed to the key cash crops of the period 1450–1750, sugar, tobacco, and coffee?

(A) They require temperate climate to grow.
(B) European indentured servants performed the labor involved in their cultivation.
(C) Revenues from the sale of these goods did not cover the costs of production and transportation.
(D) Chinese demand for all three drove expansion of these crops.
(E) Each one has addictive qualities.

273. Which of the following regional civilizations was least able to control and regulate its trade relations with the West in the period 1450–1750?

(A) Safavid Persia
(B) Tokugawa Japan
(C) Kongo kingdom
(D) Ming China
(E) Mughal India

274. Which Western power established trade forts at crucial locations in the Indian Ocean basin including Ormuz, Goa, and Malacca in the early sixteenth century?

(A) Spain
(B) England
(C) Netherlands
(D) Portugal
(E) France

275. Which was the first Asian commodity Western merchants were able to gain control over in terms of both production and trade?

(A) Cotton
(B) Opium
(C) Spices
(D) Porcelain
(E) Silk

276. The rule of which Chinese dynasties overlap with the time period
1450–1750?

   I. Yuan
  II. Ming
 III. Qing
 IV. Song

  (A) I and III
  (B) II and IV
  (C) I and IV
  (D) II and III
  (E) III and IV

277. Which three Muslim empires emerged from the wreckage left behind after
the Mongol invasions?

  (A) Umayyad, Safavid, Mughal
  (B) Mughal, Safavid, Ottoman
  (C) Abbasid, Ottoman, Umayyad
  (D) Mughal, Umayyad, Abbasid
  (E) Ottoman, Umayyad, Safavid

278. Which is the most distinguishing characteristic of the Safavid civilization
when compared to its Ottoman and Mughal empires?

  (A) High levels of palace intrigue and violent fights for succession to the
throne
  (B) Limited public roles for women
  (C) Adherence to Shia and not Sunni Islam
  (D) Growing interaction with maritime Western powers
  (E) Architectural and artistic splendor

279. Which of the following does NOT belong in a list of regions under
Ottoman control at the height of their rule in terms of territory gained?

  (A) North Africa
  (B) Middle East
  (C) Anatolia
  (D) Spain
  (E) Balkan peninsula

280. Which of the following does NOT belong in a list of characteristics of the Janissary corps in the Ottoman Empire?

(A) It was composed of young men taken from conquered lands as children and conscripted for training in military arts.

(B) It relied on gunpowder musketry and artillery for weaponry.

(C) It intervened in dynastic succession disputes more frequently over the years.

(D) It launched successful invasions of Central Europe culminating with the sack of Vienna.

(E) It carried out operations against foreign enemies and also served an internal police function.

281. Religious tolerance, Hindu-Muslim intermarriage, and abolition of the jizya head tax are all most closely associated with which Mughal ruler?

(A) Selim II

(B) Akbar

(C) Babur

(D) Aurangzeb

(E) Shah Jahan

282. Which of the following is most closely associated with the rule of Akbar the Great?

(A) State-sponsored trade missions to the New World

(B) Intensified taxation of the subcontinent's Hindu majority

(C) Assimilation of central Asian nomads into high posts in the ruling bureaucracy

(D) Prohibition of sati

(E) Lifting of the majority of the Indian population out of poverty

283. Which of the following belief systems had little to no following in India by 1750?

(A) Hinduism

(B) Islam

(C) Jainism

(D) Christianity

(E) Confucianism

284. Which destabilizing influence did the Ottoman, Mughal, and Safavid empires face in the period 1450–1750?

   (A) A growing influx of silver through trade with the West leading to widespread inflation
   (B) Revived threats from central Asian nomads
   (C) Western siege and occupation of their capital cities
   (D) Unprecedented drought
   (E) Bubonic plague outbreaks that reduced populations by one-third

285. Which development in a contemporary civilization had the greatest impact on the foreign relations of the Ottoman, Mughal, and Safavid empires in the period 1450–1750?

   (A) Movement of the maritime West toward the core of a new global trade network
   (B) Drive of the Romanov dynasty in Russia for territorial expansion
   (C) Mounting trade expeditions into the Indian Ocean basin launched by the Ming dynasty
   (D) Flooding of global markets in precious metals through massive expansion of the gold-salt trade by West African kingdoms
   (E) Polynesian settlement of Pacific Islands

286. How did rulers of the Ottoman, Safavid, and Mughal empires respond to the rising influence of the West in world affairs after 1500?

   (A) A tendency to underestimate Western capacities led to a failure to adopt Western military, technological, and scientific advances.
   (B) Highly centralized drives to confront the West on the high seas thwarted Western encroachment on trade routes and port cities.
   (C) They pursued increased diplomatic and military dependence on Ming and Qing dynasties in China to organize resistance to Western domination.
   (D) Adoption of firearms and artillery enabled coordinated assaults on the homelands of the Western merchants.
   (E) Gender roles in the Muslim empires began to more closely match Western models, in particular greater opportunities for secular education.

287. Which leadership tradition dating from the earlier caliphates continued to impact Muslim empires such as the Ottomans, Safavids, and Mughals into the period 1450–1750?
    I. Females in political power suffered crises of legitimacy due to stubborn gender norms.
    II. Lack of clear succession principles led to recurrent crises when replacing leaders.
    III. Dependence of Confucian bureaucrats undermined the authority of Islamic scholars.

    (A) I and II
    (B) II and III
    (C) I and III
    (D) I only
    (E) II only

288. Which of the following empires in the period 1450–1750 ruled the territory with the greatest degree of religious homogeneity?
    (A) Mughal
    (B) Spanish
    (C) Safavid
    (D) Ottoman
    (E) Holy Roman

289. Which of the following descriptions does NOT belong in a list of elements common to Ottoman, Safavid, and Mughal dynasties in the period 1450–1750?
    (A) Were founded by nomadic Turkic peoples
    (B) Faced mounting challenges from rising maritime Western powers
    (C) Had difficulty maintaining centralized rule over regions
    (D) Were initially dominated by warrior aristocracies
    (E) Were weakened by failed land invasions into Western Europe

290. Which civilizations were most able to pursue a policy of isolation in relation to the maritime West in the period 1450–1750?
    (A) West African
    (B) South Asian
    (C) Mesoamerican
    (D) Russian
    (E) East Asian

291. Which European trade product met with the greatest demand in East Asia in the period 1450–1750?

(A) Opium
(B) Bullion
(C) Mechanical clocks
(D) Steam engines
(E) Silk

292. Which of the following best characterizes Western presence in Africa and Asia by 1750?

(A) Westerners had toppled indigenous political powers and set up direct rule of extensive colonial holdings.
(B) Western presence was limited to coastal forts.
(C) Westerners had failed to establish a lasting presence of any sort.
(D) Substantial immigration of Europeans into Asian and African societies served as a basis for Western dominance.
(E) Conversion of a majority of Africans and Asians to Christianity made military conquest redundant.

293. Which description best characterizes the period of Ming rule in China?

(A) Turn to isolationism, consolidation of Confucian values, economic and demographic expansion
(B) Turn from isolationism, deterioration of Confucian values, economic and demographic contraction
(C) Turn from isolationism, consolidation of Confucian values, economic and demographic expansion
(D) Turn to isolationism, deterioration of Confucian values, economic and demographic contraction
(E) Turn to isolationism, deterioration of Confucian values, economic and demographic expansion

294. By 1750 what was the most populous region on the globe?

(A) Sub-Saharan Africa
(B) Western Europe
(C) East Asia
(D) South Asia
(E) North and South America

295. Which best explains the Ming decision to bring a brief period of extensive overseas exploration guided by admiral Zhenghe in the early fifteenth century to a halt?

(A) Grievous naval defeats at the hands of Portuguese maritime power

(B) Attitudes toward the expeditions within the imperial bureaucracy that ranged from indifference to hostility

(C) A rare suspension of monsoon winds that made long-distance voyages impossible

(D) Muslim dominance of the Indian Ocean basin, which led, in general, to hostility at ports of call from East Africa to Western India

(E) Growing preference of Chinese merchants and elites for goods produced in foreign lands, undermining customary notions of the superiority and centrality of China in world affairs

296. Aside from the Yuan, which other Chinese dynasty was founded by nomadic invaders?

(A) Qing (Manchu)

(B) Qin

(C) Han

(D) Song

(E) Ming

297. In which non-European society did the conversion of the local population to Christianity reach hundreds of thousands before there was a state crackdown on the new religion that accompanied a more comprehensive move toward isolation from the West?

(A) Kongo kingdom

(B) Ming China

(C) Mughal India

(D) Ottoman Empire

(E) Tokugawa Japan

298. What significance did Nagasaki Bay hold in Japanese history before the United States dropped a second atomic bomb there?

(A) It was the imperial capital of the Tokugawa regime.

(B) Invading Mongol navy was wrecked by a typhoon in a failed invasion attempt there.

(C) Matthew Perry's gunboat visit to Japan occurred here.

(D) Western trade was restricted to contact with the Dutch only at Deshima Island, allowing for limited exposure to European ideas during a period of isolation.

(E) It is the spiritual center of the indigenous Ainu people.

299. Which group made the most sustained efforts to spread Christianity in South and East Asia in the period 1450–1750?

    (A) Huguenots
    (B) Franciscans
    (C) Jesuits
    (D) Anglicans
    (E) Anabaptists

300. Which was Spain's Asian colony?

    (A) Siam
    (B) Malacca
    (C) Philippines
    (D) Java
    (E) Okinawa

CHAPTER 4

The Modern Era: 1750 to 1914

Controlling Idea: The Rise of Capitalism

Capitalism, put simply, is an economic and social system where the needs of capital come first. Capital is wealth that is invested to generate more wealth. In 1750 capitalism was in its infancy and did not shape life in a significant way outside the West and its New World colonies. By 1914 there was not a corner of the globe that had not been impacted by the growth of this dynamic new economic force. The political corollary of these economic changes was that the old feudal and monarchical systems of ruler were overthrown and undermined in a series of events that took off on a global scale in the wake of the French Revolution. The key turning point in driving such far reaching change was an Industrial Revolution made possible in the new economic, technological, and political climate fostered by the Rise of Capitalism.

301. Which of the following was a new Western motive for overseas territorial expansion in the industrial era?
 (A) Missionary drive to convert non-Western peoples to Christianity
 (B) Seizure of land to be put to use raising cash crops
 (C) Drive to dominate sources of precious minerals and metals
 (D) Need for raw materials for factory production
 (E) Access to new markets for sale of Western manufactured goods

302. How did the Dutch gain control of Java?
 (A) Massive emigration from the Netherlands to Indonesia gave the Dutch a demographic advantage.
 (B) Rapid industrialization and urbanization allowed for management of the majority of the population at work and at home.
 (C) Shrewd exploitation of existing political divisions on the island resulted in territorial concessions.
 (D) Supremacy in military technology resulted in direct rule after an initial period of warfare.
 (E) Crucial help from the Chinese navy broke the back of indigenous Javanese rulers.

303. Which rival European power did the British defeat in the eighteenth century in its drive to control the Indian subcontinent?

(A) Netherlands
(B) France
(C) Italy
(D) Spain
(E) Portugal

304. Which of the following was NOT a reason India had become Britain's most important colony by about 1800?

(A) India offered crucial port facilities for the British navy.
(B) India was a major outlet for British manufactured goods.
(C) India was an important supplier of British raw materials.
(D) India was an important location for British textile factories.
(E) Britain had lost the North American colonies.

305. During the era of British colonialism in India, why were the British content, in general, to leave Indian social hierarchies intact?

(A) Over time, exposure to Hindu doctrine on caste won British elites over.
(B) British officials were able to, in essence, graft themselves onto an existing social pyramid at its apex while incurring a minimum of social disruption.
(C) British notions of proper gender roles, such as a wife's duty to commit sati were the same as Indian ones.
(D) Superior Mughal political and military authority prevented British interference in Indian social relations.
(E) Commonplace social mobility between the caste stratifications prevalent in the subcontinent British impressed colonial administrators.

306. In which area did British and Dutch colonialists in South Asia and Indonesia assimilate the fewest indigenous practices?

(A) Religion
(B) Dress
(C) Food
(D) Housing
(E) Work habits

307. By what method did Western imperialists work to gain a dependable corps of local managers to aid in the administration of their colonies?

  I. Kidnapping of managers' family members and holding them for ransom

  II. Conversion of local elites to Christianity

  III. Education of new generations of colonized youth in Western languages and cultural practices

  (A) I and II

  (B) II and III

  (C) I and III

  (D) II only

  (E) III only

308. Which event highlighted widespread corruption and mismanagement among British East India Company administrators?

  (A) Robert Clive's victory at the Battle of Plassey in 1757

  (B) Chaotic departure of British forces in 1947

  (C) Decision to fire on unarmed crowds at Amritsar in 1918

  (D) Famine in Bengal in the 1770s

  (E) Rowlatt Act of 1918

309. Which reform was most emblematic of growing British interest in transforming Indian social relations in the nineteenth century?

  (A) Dismantling of the caste system

  (B) Prohibition of sati

  (C) Expansion of education for girls

  (D) Building interest in the sport of cricket

  (E) Construction of trade schools to train a new Indian industrial working class

310. Which answer choice contains the major rivals to British industrial and imperial supremacy that emerged in the second half of the nineteenth century?

  (A) China, Belgium, Germany, the United States

  (B) The United States, Brazil, France, Germany

  (C) China, Brazil, Germany, Belgium

  (D) The United States, Belgium, France, Germany

  (E) France, Germany, Brazil, Belgium

311. Which of the following factors best describes international relations among the Western powers in the decades leading up to 1914?
    I. Rivalry involving colonial spoils, arms races, and alliance formation
    II. Major direct military clashes in colonial portions of the globe
    III. Mutual disinterest in territorial and military advances

    (A) I and II
    (B) II and III
    (C) I and III
    (D) I only
    (E) II only

312. Which answer choice contains regions that were nominally independent but nonetheless endured significant Western informal political and economic influence by 1914?

    (A) West Africa, South Asia, China, Latin America
    (B) China, Persia, the Middle East, Latin America
    (C) Persia, West Africa, South Asia, Latin America
    (D) South Asia, the Middle East, China, Latin America
    (E) West Africa, Persia, the Middle East, Latin America

313. Which of the following does NOT belong in a list of contested settler societies?

    (A) Algeria
    (B) India
    (C) South Africa
    (D) Kenya
    (E) Hawaii

314. Which of the following is generally true of indigenous individuals promoted to assist Western imperialists in their rule of the colony?

    (A) When possible, Christians were chosen.
    (B) They tended to be from minority ethnic groups.
    (C) They were given limited Western education and technical training.
    (D) They were barred from the very top supervisory ranks.
    (E) All of the above

315. Which of the following best characterizes the difference between educational systems set up by imperialists in Africa and India?

    (A) African colonies contained comparatively more schools administered by colonial governments than India.

    (B) African schools tended to be set up by Christian missionaries while Indian ones were set up by the colonial state.

    (C) Indian education mainly consisted of trade schools for training industrial workers, while African schools did not.

    (D) African education mainly consisted of trade schools for training industrial workers, while Indian schools did not.

    (E) White supremacist notions dissuaded imperialists from setting up education in either colony.

316. Which sector of the colonized economy had experienced the least expansion by 1914?

    (A) Transport

    (B) Mining

    (C) Export crop cultivation

    (D) Heavy industrial capacity

    (E) Raw material extraction

317. The purpose of the Berlin Conference of 1885 was

    (A) For representatives of Western industry to learn cutting-edge German industrial techniques

    (B) For representatives of colonized peoples to learn cutting-edge German industrial techniques

    (C) To set quotas and agreements surrounding the growth of the German navy

    (D) To negotiate settlements among Western rivalries over the partition of Africa

    (E) To study the ideas of the philosopher Friedrich Nietzsche

318. The India Congress Party's early membership consisted heavily of middle-class individuals, including M. K. Gandhi, trained in which profession?

    (A) Journalism

    (B) Engineering

    (C) Law

    (D) Policing

    (E) Civil administration

319. Which choice lays out the correct order in which the Industrial Revolution began and spread?

(A) Great Britain, United States, continental Europe
(B) Continental Europe, United States, Great Britain,
(C) United States, continental Europe, Great Britain
(D) Great Britain, continental Europe, United States
(E) Continental Europe, Great Britain, United States

320. Which of the following ran counter to the democratic impulses associated with the American Revolution?

(A) Rejection of aristocratic notions of hierarchy in the thirteen colonies
(B) Continued centrality of slavery to the colonial socioeconomic order
(C) New England's tradition of town meetings
(D) Virginia's practice of election of a House of Burgesses
(E) Demands for representation in British Parliament

321. Which list places key events of the French Revolution in proper chronological order?

(A) Formation of National Assembly, Reign of Terror, Directory, rule of Napoleon
(B) Reign of Terror, rule of Napoleon, formation of National Assembly, Directory
(C) Directory, rule of Napoleon, formation of National Assembly, Reign of Terror
(D) Formation of National Assembly, Reign of Terror, rule of Napoleon, Directory
(E) Rule of Napoleon, Directory, Reign of Terror, Formation of National Assembly

322. Which of the following documents spells out Enlightenment ideas as they were applied to revolutionary France?

(A) The Declaration of Independence
(B) *Second Treatise of Government*
(C) *The Social Contract*
(D) *Declaration of the Rights of Man and Citizen*
(E) *Eighteenth Brumaire of Louis Bonaparte*

323. Which group emerged at the peak of French social status as a result of the French Revolution?
   (A) Urban proletariat and artisans
   (B) Aristocracy
   (C) Clergy
   (D) Bourgeoisie
   (E) Peasantry

324. Which statement best characterizes the response of ruling elites in neighboring Western powers to the toppling of the French monarchy?
   I. Indifference
   II. Military intervention
   III. Imitation
   (A) I only
   (B) II only
   (C) III only
   (D) I and II
   (E) II and III

325. Historians estimate the numbers of victims in the Reign of Terror in roughly what figures?
   (A) Hundreds
   (B) Thousands
   (C) Tens of thousands
   (D) Hundreds of thousands
   (E) Millions

326. Which traditions of the French Revolution did not survive long beyond the initial and radical phases?
   (A) Equality under the law
   (B) Attack on feudal privilege and institutions
   (C) Popular nationalism
   (D) The metric system
   (E) Women's leading role in toppling established political powers

327. Which nineteenth-century political ideology stressed principles of laissez-faire and constitutional rule?

(A) Conservative
(B) Liberal
(C) Fascist
(D) Anarchist
(E) Socialist

328. Which answer choice includes the major political groupings in nineteenth-century Europe?

(A) Conservative, liberal, radical
(B) Liberal, radical, fascist
(C) Fascist, conservative, radical
(D) Radical, fascist, anarchist
(E) Liberal, fascist, conservative

329. Which of the following Western societies escaped internal disturbances during the Revolutions of 1848?

(A) Germany
(B) Austria
(C) Hungary
(D) Russia
(E) France

330. Which of the Western societies expanded democratic rights in the first half of the nineteenth century but did not experience the mass upheavals of 1848?

   I. Great Britain
   II. France
   III. The United States

(A) I and II
(B) II and III
(C) I and III
(D) I, II, and III
(E) III only

331. Which of the following was NOT an influential political force in Europe by the late nineteenth century?

(A) Feminism
(B) Social democracy
(C) Socialism
(D) Anarchism
(E) Absolute monarchy

332. Which of the following does NOT belong in a list of new responsibilities Western governments gained in the nineteenth century?

(A) Public education
(B) Workplace safety regulation
(C) Child labor regulation
(D) Minimum-wage regulation
(E) Mass conscription

333. Who does NOT belong in a list of nineteenth- and early twentieth-century rationalist thinkers?

(A) Karl Marx
(B) Albert Einstein
(C) Sigmund Freud
(D) Charles Darwin
(E) John Locke

334. Among Western settler societies, which had emerged as the leading industrial power by 1914?

(A) Canada
(B) New Zealand
(C) Australia
(D) The United States
(E) Mexico

335. Which of the following did most to set the United States apart as unique within Western civilizations in the nineteenth century?

(A) Persistence of racialized slavery
(B) Levels of urbanization
(C) Industrial development
(D) Territorial size
(E) Federal political system

336. The rise of which industrial power in the decades leading to 1914 upset the established diplomatic and economic order among Western powers that had existed throughout much of the nineteenth century?

(A) France
(B) Great Britain
(C) Germany
(D) Sweden
(E) Switzerland

337. Which answer choice best captures the changes historians associate with what is termed the "second industrial revolution"?

(A) Industrialization outside of England
(B) Shift to nuclear power in the West after World War II
(C) Central role of heavy industry and electrical power
(D) Rapid urbanization associated with factory production
(E) Move to an "information economy" after the rise of the personal computer

338. Upon which demand would radicals and liberals have most likely agreed?

(A) Worker control of industry
(B) Minimum-wage laws
(C) Expansion of voting rights
(D) A graduated income tax
(E) Return of monarchy

339. Which of the following causes did the American and French Revolutions share?

  I. Frustration over high levels of taxation
 II. Resentment at exclusion from governmental decision making
III. Anger sparked by feudal exploitation of the peasantry

(A) I and II
(B) II and III
(C) I and III
(D) I only
(E) II only

340. Which of the following is a consequence and not a precondition of industrial development?

    (A) Capital accumulation
    (B) Abundant labor supply
    (C) Organized labor union movement
    (D) Technical know-how
    (E) Access to raw materials

341. Which thinker is most closely associated with formulating the theories of "Social Darwinism"?

    (A) Karl Marx
    (B) Jean-Jacques Rousseau
    (C) Thomas Hobbes
    (D) Herbert Spencer
    (E) Charles Darwin

342. Which group of formerly colonized nations gained political independence from Western colonialism in the nineteenth century?

    (A) Ghana, Mexico, India
    (B) Argentina, Mexico, Brazil
    (C) India, Mexico, Brazil
    (D) Brazil, India, Ghana
    (E) Argentina, Mexico, Ghana

343. Which situation did formally independent Latin American nations have most in common with colonized portions of Africa and Asia in the nineteenth century?

    (A) Rapidly expanding social, economic, and political possibilities for the majority of women
    (B) A dependent position in the world economy due to the rise of Western industrial capitalism
    (C) Declining importance of race and ethnicity in defining social status
    (D) Supplantation of agriculture by industry as the main occupation of the laboring population
    (E) Depopulation due to exposure to new diseases brought by Western colonialists

344. Which of the following concerns made Creole elites, who yearned for independence from Spain, what we might call "cautious revolutionaries"?

(A) Fear that the Spanish monarchs were more capable rulers
(B) Fear that continued rapid industrialization would create urban instability
(C) A growing communist threat inspired by the example of the Bolshevik Revolution in the Soviet Union
(D) Fear that slaves and other oppressed groups would target local elites as part of a general social upheaval
(E) Fear that women would reject subordination in the private and public spheres if independence were achieved

345. After the United States, which was the next New World colony to gain independence from European power?

(A) Mexico
(B) Argentina
(C) Brazil
(D) Haiti
(E) Cuba

346. Which event in Europe contributed most directly to the wave of independence struggle in early nineteenth-century Latin America?

(A) Publication of the Gutenberg bible
(B) The Reconquista
(C) Napoleon's invasion of Spain
(D) Fascist aerial bombardment of Guernica
(E) Onset of World War I

347. Why was the struggle for Brazilian independence distinctive in Latin American history?

(A) Brazil was the only colony whose economy was dependent on cash crops.
(B) Brazil remained a monarchy after independence.
(C) Brazil abolished slavery before independence was achieved.
(D) Brazil was the first colony to achieve independence.
(E) Brazil was the only ethnically diverse colony where racial hierarchy did not exist before or after independence.

348. Which social practices of the early United States were replicated in newly independent Spanish Latin America?

(A) Slavery was maintained.

(B) Women remained subordinate to men.

(C) Property restrictions were placed on voting.

(D) Established colonial elites moved to the top ranks of political power.

(E) All of the above

349. Which is the best reason why rail networks were underdeveloped in Spanish Latin America at the time independence was achieved?

(A) Colonial-era Latin American mining was not profitable enough to warrant rail investment.

(B) No cash crops were produced for export.

(C) Rail technology was relatively new and limited to small areas of Britain, Western Europe, and the United States at the time.

(D) Latin American mountains and rivers made rail construction impossible.

(E) Rail technology had yet to be invented.

350. What impact did the instability of the wars for independence have on subsequent developments in Latin America?

(A) Agricultural regions devastated by modern warfare were slow to recover, leading to widespread famine.

(B) Female veterans of military service refused subordinate roles in the home.

(C) Military leaders remained influential and intervened frequently in political affairs.

(D) Mestizo, slave, and indigenous populations formed guerrilla units and launched armed struggle for communism.

(E) The grip of the Catholic church was weakened and various strains of Protestantism became the dominant form of Christianity.

351. Which set of opposing political groupings would be most likely to disagree chiefly over the power of local versus national government?

(A) Fascist and Communist

(B) Democrat and Republican

(C) Anarchist and Liberal

(D) Centralist and Federalist

(E) Liberal and Conservative

352. What was the main commonality Liberal and Conservative politicians shared in nineteenth-century Latin America?

(A) They agreed that the Catholic church had too much power.

(B) Both were led by wealthy landowners and the urban middle to upper classes.

(C) They agreed on the immediate abolition of slavery and repatriation to Africa.

(D) Both looked with admiration on the example of independent Haiti.

(E) Both were influenced by the ideas of Karl Marx.

353. What best characterizes relations between newly independent Latin American nations and British power in the mid-nineteenth century?

(A) Mutual indifference

(B) British indifference to Latin American requests for alliance

(C) British naval assistance in defense of Latin American independence in exchange for access to Latin American consumer markets and raw materials

(D) Latin American trade protectionism in the face of British exports to stimulate local industrial development

(E) Unified diplomatic and military action centered around suppression of the transatlantic slave trade

354. Which area of the Latin American economy was most damaged by free-trade relations with the British?

(A) Rail

(B) Port city

(C) Manufacturing

(D) Ranching

(E) Agricultural

355. Which does NOT belong in a list of the most important Latin American exports to the industrial West in the second half of the nineteenth century?

(A) Beef

(B) Coffee

(C) Grains

(D) Guano

(E) Gold

356. War with which Western power reduced Mexico's territory by about half?

    (A) The United States

    (B) France

    (C) Spain

    (D) Portugal

    (E) Germany

357. Which choice best characterizes the top priorities of the liberal regime of Mexican leader Benito Juarez?

    (A) Constitutional rule with reduced privileges for church and military elites

    (B) Land reform to satisfy the needs of an impoverished peasantry

    (C) Maintenance of privileges for church and military elites

    (D) Rapid industrialization by way of a planned economic system

    (E) Military action to regain territory recently lost in the Mexican-American War

358. Which independent Latin American nation saw the defeat of the last unassimilated indigenous group willing to take up armed struggle to defend its autonomy?

    (A) Argentina

    (B) Mexico

    (C) Cuba

    (D) Venezuela

    (E) Colombia

359. Which Latin American nation attracted the greatest number of European immigrants in the late nineteenth and early twentieth centuries?

    (A) Colombia

    (B) Peru

    (C) Venezuela

    (D) Mexico

    (E) Argentina

360. Which best characterizes the rule and impact of Porfirio Diaz in Mexico?

(A) Sacrifice of liberal political principles in pursuit of industrial and infrastructural modernization

(B) Peasant-based populist mandate achieving comprehensive land reform

(C) Puppet ruler manipulated by German imperialism bringing little to no economic development

(D) Conservative ruler who returned large landowners and Catholic elites to power

(E) Communist revolutionary implementing a series of Five-Year Plans for agriculture and industry

361. Where did U.S. influence expand most greatly as a result of the Spanish-American War?

(A) Mexico

(B) Cuba

(C) Puerto Rico

(D) A and B

(E) B and C

362. Which Latin American nation lost Panama to a U.S.-backed revolution after it refused to bend to U.S. demands in the construction of a canal there?

(A) Venezuela

(B) Guatemala

(C) Honduras

(D) Colombia

(E) Mexico

363. In which Latin American nation did indigenous people play the most prominent political role during and after the winning of independence?

(A) Argentina

(B) Colombia

(C) Brazil

(D) Mexico

(E) Cuba

364. Which statement best characterizes Ottoman and Qing Chinese relations with the West by about 1750?

(A) Both empires were in full military retreat and subject to carrying out Western economic demands.

(B) Both empires were successfully carrying out policies of isolation from the West.

(C) Qing China was able to strongly regulate relations with the West while Ottoman rulers were less able to repel Western incursions into their territorial waters.

(D) Qing China pursued a policy of imitation of Western industrial and mercantile practices while Ottoman rulers refused to do so.

(E) Both empires had launched effective counterattacks culminating with occupation of key Western urban centers.

365. A long period of Ottoman territorial retreat ended with the birth of which modern nation?

(A) Iran

(B) Pakistan

(C) Turkey

(D) Egypt

(E) Serbia

366. Initial expansion of Western-style university systems, communication methods, railways, and newspaper production and the promulgation of a European-style constitution are associated with which period in the history of the Ottoman Empire?

(A) World War I era

(B) Era of Suleyman the Magnificent

(C) Great Depression era

(D) Tanzimat reform era

(E) Crusades era

367. The nineteenth-century Egyptian political leader Muhammad Ali is best known for

(A) Revitalization of Islamic fundamentalism in the Ottoman world

(B) Defeat of the British navy to prevent Greek independence

(C) Determined but ultimately unsuccessful efforts to modernize Egypt's economy along Western lines

(D) Breaking Egyptian dependence on cotton exports in trade relations

(E) Defeating Napoleon's invasion of Egypt

368. Which of the following made Egypt an attractive target for Western imperialist expansion in the late nineteenth century?

(A) Gold deposits
(B) Control of Nile River trade
(C) Lucrative tourism prospects
(D) Construction and control of the Suez Canal
(E) Fertile land of the Nile River delta

369. Which of the following does not belong in a list of policies generally followed by a rising Chinese dynasty?

(A) Repair and expansion of dams, canals, and roads
(B) Lowering tax burdens for the peasantry
(C) Expanding opportunities for peasants to own land
(D) Strengthening of civil service examination systems
(E) Concentration of land ownership into ever fewer hands

370. Which of the following best describes China's trade relations with the rest of the world by about 1750?

(A) Export of Chinese manufactured and luxury goods in exchange for Western manufactured and luxury goods
(B) Export of Chinese manufactured and luxury goods in exchange for silver
(C) Import of Western manufactured and luxury goods in exchange for silver
(D) Negligible levels of trade with the rest of the world since China produced all it needed
(E) Mercantilist expansion colonizing the Philippines, Indonesia, and Southeast Asia

371. Which of the following does NOT belong in a list of nineteenth-century challenges to the rule of the Qing dynasty in China?

(A) Floods
(B) Peasant rebellion
(C) Foreign invasion
(D) Corruption in the bureaucracy
(E) Expanding influence of communism in China

372. Which statement best captures the ruling Qing dynasty's attitude toward the West particularly in the period before the Opium Wars?

(A) Western civilization possessed military and industrial practices worthy of emulation.

(B) Western civilization posed a mortal threat to Chinese civilization.

(C) Western civilization was just another barbarian foreign society.

(D) Western civilization possessed artistic and intellectual practices worthy of emulation.

(E) Western civilization allowed for gender roles worthy of emulation.

373. Which of the following best explains the reason the British turned to trading opium in China?

(A) Firsthand experience supplying mass opium addiction in the thirteen colonies proved the profitability of the trade.

(B) British merchants could find no other commodity the Chinese needed.

(C) Successful expansion of the opium trade in India provided a model for replication.

(D) Imperialist designs for direct rule in China would be more easily attainable over a population pacified by narcotics.

(E) British monarchs wanted to share the benefits of widespread medical and recreational use of opium they had experienced in British society with the Chinese.

374. Land redistribution, reforms to simplify Chinese writing, equality for women, and armed struggle were major features of which pair of Chinese movements?

(A) Taiping Rebellion, Communist

(B) May Fourth Movement, Taiping Rebellion

(C) Nationalist, Taiping Rebellion

(D) May Fourth Movement, Communist

(E) Nationalist, Boxer Rebellion

375. Which does NOT belong in a group of nations that had achieved territorial concessions in China by 1914?

(A) Japan

(B) Germany

(C) Britain

(D) France

(E) Italy

376. Which of the following does NOT belong in a list of Chinese movements resentful of foreign domination?

(A) Boxer Rebellion
(B) May Fourth Movement
(C) Tanzimat Reform Movement
(D) Chinese Communist Movement
(E) Kuomintang (Nationalist) Movement

377. Which of the following is NOT a reason Chinese civilization suffered a more total collapse in the face of Western pressure than Muslim civilization had by 1914?

(A) Muslims had faced conflict with the West since the birth of their religion and hence were more accustomed to it, while the shock of Western interference was more abrupt for the Chinese.
(B) Muslims were not bound to defend a single state, while the Chinese destiny was linked to the survival of the Qing dynasty.
(C) Muslim civilization was concentrated in a more densely populated and urbanized manner and better suited to coastal or naval defense than the more rural and inland Chinese population.
(D) Muslim rulers were somewhat accustomed to exchange of knowledge with the West while the Chinese elites tended to view outsiders as barbarians one and all.
(E) Disparate Muslim peoples could unite around their faith while the Chinese lacked a similar homegrown universal religious tradition.

378. Which Chinese imperial bureaucrat wrote a famous letter to Queen Victoria demanding a cessation of British shipment of opium into China?

(A) Lin Zexu
(B) Qianlong
(C) Sun Yat-sen
(D) Pu Yi
(E) Hong Xiuquan

379. How were Qing dynasty-era ethnic Han Chinese men forced to show respect for their Manchu rulers?

    (A) All Chinese males removed themselves from posts in the civil service bureaucracy to make way for Manchu officials.

    (B) Each Chinese male had to carry out a self-financed pilgrimage to the Forbidden City to pay homage to the emperor.

    (C) Each male sent his first daughter through a selection process for the imperial concubines.

    (D) Chinese males were forced to wear the distinctive queue hairstyle.

    (E) Chinese males were forced to abandon agriculture and work in Manchu factories.

380. Which traditional element of dynastic decline faced by the Qing dynasty in the late nineteenth century was most different from earlier instances of the same phenomenon?

    (A) Peasant rebellion

    (B) Natural disaster

    (C) Foreign invasion

    (D) Political decentralization

    (E) Imperial corruption and decadence

381. Which challenge to Manchu rule is least attributable to changes brought about by the emergence of the West as a global power and trade intermediary?

    (A) Increased opium addiction

    (B) Japanese aggression

    (C) Yellow River floods of unprecedented devastation

    (D) Massive population growth

    (E) Silver inflation

382. Which pair of regional powers was able, by 1914, to initiate substantial industrialization and resist Western domination?

    (A) Ottoman Empire and South Africa

    (B) Russia and Japan

    (C) South Africa and Russia

    (D) Ottoman Empire and Japan

    (E) Argentina and Ottoman Empire

383. Which common trait helps to explain Russian and Japanese ability to modernize in the nineteenth century?

(A) Extensive experience with cultural imitation, Russia imitating Byzantium and the West, Japan imitating China

(B) Prior adoption and variation of Christian teachings, providing a basis for westernization

(C) Royal appreciation of the democratic tradition

(D) Presence of abundant natural resources, particularly coal and iron ore deposits, within traditional territorial confines

(E) Preexisting traditions of widespread public education and literacy

384. All of the following statements are reasons monarchy survived so much longer in Russia than it did anywhere else in Europe EXCEPT

(A) The defeat of Napoleon in 1812 seemed to indicate a royal power could beat a modern one.

(B) Serfdom continued to provide a stable labor system.

(C) Czarist autocracy insulated Russia from the uprisings of 1830 and 1848 in much of Europe.

(D) Czars were able to mobilize enough industrial development to remain a world power.

(E) The Romanov dynasty imitated the stable British model of constitutional monarchy.

385. Which of the following decisions by Russian czars was motivated by a long-held desire for a warm-water port and access to the trade of the Mediterranean Sea?

(A) Construction of the trans-Siberian railway

(B) Launching the Crimean War

(C) Construction of St. Petersburg

(D) Launching the Russo-Japanese War

(E) Annexation of Poland

386. Which of the following choices contains an accurate list of nineteenth-century reforms carried out by Russian czars?

(A) Collectivization of agriculture, emancipation of the serfs, establishment of zemstvos

(B) Construction of trans-Siberian railway, construction of St. Petersburg, establishment of zemstvos

(C) Establishment of zemstvos, construction of trans-Siberian railway, emancipation of the serfs

(D) Emancipation of the serfs, collectivization of agriculture, construction of the trans-Siberian railway

(E) Collectivization of agriculture, establishment of zemstvos, construction of the trans-Siberian railway

387. Which of the following was experienced by Russia and not Japan by 1914?

(A) Mass revolutionary upheaval

(B) Rapid urbanization

(C) State-directed industrial development

(D) Expansion of educational opportunity

(E) War for territorial acquisition

388. Which of the following was the main reform put in place as a result of the 1905 Revolution in Russia?

(A) Unions were legalized.

(B) Freedom of the press was established.

(C) A national representative assembly, the Duma, was created.

(D) Czarism was abandoned in favor of representative democracy.

(E) Agriculture was collectivized.

389. In the decades leading to 1914, how were Japanese imperial designs for Asia and Russian imperial designs in Eastern Europe similar?

(A) Each posed itself as the natural leader of a broader and ethnically similar mass of people.

(B) Both aimed at access to raw materials and/or consumer markets.

(C) Each had annexed adjacent territory and made it a formal colony.

(D) A and B

(E) A and C

390. How was the opening of Japan to the West different from other encounters between major civilizations and the West around the world in the period 1750–1914?

(A) French imperialists who dominated Japan refused to confer citizenry on the Japanese as they had in Africa.

(B) Japanese ruling elites remained in continuous control of the pace and terms of relations with the West.

(C) Japan was the only major civilization whose first contact with the West was with the United States.

(D) Japanese military power was able to thwart Western intervention.

(E) Exposure of the Japanese to Christianity created a minority community that assisted in direct colonial rule by the British.

391. What was the role of the Meiji Restoration in Japanese history?

(A) Strengthening of the power of the Tokugawa Shogunate

(B) Expansion of Chinese influence in Japanese society

(C) Reversal of traditional Japanese gender norms

(D) Launching of Japan on a course of modernization and westernization

(E) Reconstruction of Japan after the devastation of the Second World War

392. Which of the following best describes the political system set up in Japan during the Meiji Restoration?

(A) Proletarian dictatorship

(B) Democratic republic

(C) Constitutional monarchy

(D) Feudal state

(E) Absolute monarchy

393. How did industrial development in Japan and Russia tend to differ from similar processes in Western Europe and the United States?

(A) Industrial development was not applied to military purposes.

(B) Industrial development did not spur territorial expansion.

(C) Industrial development tended to be more state-directed.

(D) Industrial development was more dependent on immigrant labor.

(E) Industrial development led to the rise of an organized labor movement, and unions were legalized.

394. In which area did westernization of Japan have the least impact?

(A) Politics
(B) Religion
(C) Economy
(D) Fashion
(E) Science

395. Why was the Russo-Japanese war a significant turning point in world history?

(A) It was the first conflict decided by battle at sea.
(B) It was the first conflict where mass-produced weaponry was employed.
(C) The rifled musket was used for the first time.
(D) Iron-hulled ships were used for the first time.
(E) A non-Western power defeated a modern European power in battle.

396. Which of the following nations pursued a course of overseas territorial expansion only after beginning the process of industrialization?

(A) Netherlands
(B) Great Britain
(C) Spain
(D) Japan
(E) France

397. Which of the following regions incorporated Western ideas in the nineteenth century but did not manage to achieve political independence from the West?

(A) Russia
(B) Japan
(C) Mexico
(D) India
(E) Brazil

398. Which best describes the initial method of British rule over its Indian colony?

  I. Popular representative assemblies were established to include the Indian population in decision making.
  II. Direct rule by Queen Elizabeth was established.
  III. East India Trading Company officials set up favorable relations for the British with local ruling elites.

  (A) I and II
  (B) II and III
  (C) I and III
  (D) II only
  (E) III only

399. Which inventor is most closely associated with the invention of the steam engine?

  (A) Thomas Edison
  (B) George Washington Carver
  (C) Eli Whitney
  (D) James Watt
  (E) George Stephenson

400. All of the following were important figures in Latin American independence movements EXCEPT

  (A) Agustin Iturbide
  (B) Miguel de Hidalgo
  (C) Simon Bolivar
  (D) Jose de San Martin
  (E) Emiliano Zapata

CHAPTER 5

The Present Era: 1914 to Present

Controlling Idea: An "Age of Extremes"

Dr. Eric Hobsbawm (Emeritus Professor at Birkbeck College, University of London and the New School in New York City) titled his excellent book on the "short twentieth century," 1914–1991, the *Age of Extremes*, and this phrase is a useful way to begin to conceptualize the dizzying scope and pace of change we have seen in the years since the opening shots of the First World War in 1914. Where before we had wars now we have had world wars. Where before we had powers now we have seen superpowers. The explosion of technological innovation and productive capacity we saw in the Industrial Revolution has been expanded upon in ways individuals alive in 1914 could scarcely dream of. Yet all too familiar, in point of fact ancient, patterns of poverty still define life for billions of people. It is, then, an "Age of Extremes" in wealth and poverty and an "Age of Extremes" for the biosphere where we have reached the situation in which man-made gases contribute to planetary climate change.

401. Which of the following best characterizes developments in the societies of Western Europe in the decades after World War II?
   I. Expanding welfare state provisions
   II. Steady economic growth
   III. Broad enthusiasm for expansion of colonial holdings

(A) I only
(B) I and II
(C) I and III
(D) II only
(E) II and III

402. Which political system, discredited by its inability to effectively prevent economic collapse or a turn to political extremism, emerged triumphant in the post–World War II West?

(A) Socialism
(B) Liberal democracy
(C) Fascism
(D) Monarchy
(E) Authoritarian populism

403. Which nation emerged as the preeminent force in the West after World War II?

(A) England
(B) France
(C) United States
(D) West Germany
(E) Japan

404. Which of the following phrases is most closely associated with the guarantee of U.S. protection from Soviet aggression offered to Western Europe and Japan during the Cold War era?

(A) Détente
(B) Nuclear umbrella
(C) Isolationism
(D) Berlin airlift
(E) Multilateralism

405. The North Atlantic Treaty Organization (NATO) and the Warsaw Pact are most accurately described as

I. Free trade zones
II. Collective security organizations
III. Colonial holdings

(A) I and II
(B) II and III
(C) I and III
(D) II only
(E) III only

406. Nikita Khrushchev is best known for

(A) Repudiation of repressive measures taken during the Stalin era
(B) Abandonment of Five-Year Plans and collective farms
(C) Glasnost
(D) Starving Soviet scientists of resources necessary to match Western achievements
(E) Perestroika

407. Which socialist Eastern European nation was not a Soviet satellite state?

(A) Romania
(B) Hungary
(C) East Germany
(D) Yugoslavia
(E) Bulgaria

408. Which of the following was NOT a characteristic of the Soviet economy after World War II?

(A) Source of massive environmental damage
(B) Generally unresponsive to demand for consumer goods
(C) Incapable of significant arms production
(D) Centrally planned
(E) Inefficient, particularly in agriculture

409. Which U.S. general is most closely associated with a program of economic assistance to Western European nations struggling to rebuild after World War II?

(A) Adlai Stevenson
(B) Dwight Eisenhower
(C) George Patton
(D) Douglas MacArthur
(E) George Marshall

410. In which of the following cases did the United States provide aid to break a Soviet blockade?

(A) U-2 incident
(B) Bay of Pigs invasion
(C) Berlin airlift
(D) Marshall Plan
(E) Crimean War

411. The United States imposed all of the following elements on Japanese state and society after World War II EXCEPT

(A) Separation of legislative and executive powers
(B) Strict secular government, banning Shintoism as state religion
(C) Land reform
(D) Women's suffrage
(E) Banning labor unions

412. On what continent did the United States fight its two largest conflicts of the Cold War era?

(A) Europe
(B) Asia
(C) Africa
(D) Australia
(E) South America

413. Which was true of both the Korean War and the Vietnam War?
  I. During the war the United States fought a communist North from base areas in a U.S.-friendly South.
  II. U.S. opponents received direct aid from the USSR and/or China.
  III. U.S. forces operated under a UN mandate.

(A) I and II
(B) II and III
(C) I and III
(D) II only
(E) I only

414. Which was true of the Korean War but not the Vietnam War?
  I. Conflict resulted in a lasting U.S. occupation.
  II. Conflict resulted in unification of North and South under communist rule.
  III. U.S. commanding officers argued for the use of nuclear weapons against the enemy.

(A) I and II
(B) II and III
(C) I and III
(D) II only
(E) I only

415. Mao's campaign to infuse industrial development into the national economy at the commune level was called

(A) New Democracy
(B) Protracted Warfare
(C) "Hundred Flowers" Period
(D) The Long March
(E) The Great Leap Forward

416. Which formerly colonized country has taken the most drastic measures to limit population growth?

(A) Mexico
(B) Nigeria
(C) India
(D) China
(E) Egypt

417. The "Great Revolution for a Proletarian Culture" in China is best described as

(A) A massive Deng Xiaoping–era program for technical training of peasants in industrial techniques
(B) The strategic retreat during the 1930s led by Mao Zedong from southern China to base areas to the north and west
(C) A 1960s–era campaign where mass mobilizations of youth were employed to target and repress "capitalist roaders" in positions of authority and continue the violent revolutionary struggle for a communist society
(D) Student demonstrations for political reform in 1989 brutally suppressed by Chinese authorities
(E) Present-day migration of rural workers into industrializing zones along the coast to labor in factories producing consumer goods for export

418. Which of the following is NOT among the "Four Modernizations" put forward by Deng Xiaoping as key to economic self-reliance and emergence of China as a world power by the early twenty-first century?

(A) Agriculture
(B) Industry
(C) Science and technology
(D) Classless society
(E) National defense

419. Which of the following best characterizes developments in China since 1979?

   I. Massive internal migration
  II. Strong export-driven economic growth
 III. Multiparty elections

(A) I and II
(B) II and III
(C) I and III
(D) II only
(E) III only

420. Neocolonialism is best defined as

(A) Western efforts to expand colonial holdings after the Second World War
(B) The ongoing situation of economic dependency that afflicts "Third World" even after decolonization
(C) The post–World War II population boom in "Third World"
(D) A description of the Soviet relationship with satellite states of Eastern Europe during the Cold War
(E) All colonization that occurred after Latin American nations won independence from Spain

421. Which is an impact of population growth in the developing world?

(A) Declining importance of the International Monetary Fund in the global economy
(B) Falling numbers of refugees
(C) Rapid and haphazard urbanization
(D) Rising status for females
(E) Reduced pollution levels

422. Which goal did nationalist leaders find most difficult to achieve upon gaining independence?

(A) Economic development and jobs for all
(B) Maintenance of territorial integrity of the new nations
(C) Participation in world trade
(D) Membership in the United Nations
(E) Establishment of secular government

423. Which was the most typical response of nationalist leaders in developing countries to popular unrest connected to persistent poverty and/or ethnic strife?

(A) Requests for the return of Western colonial management
(B) A turn to military dictatorship
(C) Free and fair elections of new leaders capable of resolving major grievances
(D) Establishment of new international borders to appease minority ethnicities
(E) The launching of armed struggle against established elites and the setting up of socialist regimes

424. Who was the leader of the first sub-Saharan nation to gain independence?

(A) Jomo Kenyatta
(B) Nelson Mandela
(C) Gamal Abdel Nasser
(D) Mobutu Sese Seko
(E) Kwame Nkrumah

425. Which of the following is NOT a trend or event associated with developments in post–WWII Egypt?

(A) Expulsion of the British from the Suez Canal Zone
(B) Construction of the Aswan dam
(C) Growth of Islamic fundamentalism
(D) Establishment of state-subsidized public education
(E) Successful import-substitution industrialization

426. Which of the following accurately summarizes developments in India since independence?

I. Maintenance of civilian rule and representative democracy
II. Growth of a middle class and information technology sector
III. Elimination of caste distinctions
IV. Penetration of Green Revolution agricultural techniques down to the village level

(A) I and IV
(B) II and III
(C) I, II, and III
(D) I only
(E) I, II, and IV

427. Which of the following statements about the Iranian Revolution of 1979 is most accurate?

(A) It marked the end of British colonialism in Iran.
(B) It overthrew a monarchy and installed a liberal democracy.
(C) It was guided by a non-Western ideology.
(D) It was welcomed by neighboring nations.
(E) Its leaders withdrew Iran from the Organization of Petroleum Exporting Countries (OPEC).

428. Which of the following was the only newly independent nation to experience civil war secession and the formation of another nation within decades of decolonization?

(A) Sudan
(B) South Africa
(C) Mexico
(D) Pakistan
(E) Nigeria

429. Which natural resource or crop have developing nations been able to trade in the global economy on terms most favorable to themselves?

(A) Cocoa
(B) Coffee
(C) Oil
(D) Diamonds
(E) Aluminum

430. Why was South Africa's independence struggle atypical when compared with most other African nations?

(A) Few other African nations gained independence in the 1960s.
(B) South Africa embarked on a program of rapid state-directed industrialization soon after achieving independence.
(C) Independence was negotiated by a South African government that consisted of white settlers only.
(D) South Africa nationalized gold and diamond mines and directed profits from their operation into development projects to lift the standard of living of the black majority there.
(E) South Africa's independence movement was led by women.

431. Nelson Mandela and Steven Biko are associated with the struggle against what?

(A) Soviet socialism
(B) South African apartheid
(C) U.S. imperialism
(D) French colonialism
(E) German fascism

432. Which West African nation boasts the continent's largest population and substantial oil reserves?

(A) Senegal
(B) Ghana
(C) Ethiopia
(D) Congo
(E) Nigeria

433. Which of the following was the first group targeted by the Nazis for repression once they seized power in Germany?

(A) Jews
(B) Communists
(C) Gypsies
(D) Homosexuals
(E) Small-business men

434. Who was the first fascist dictator?

(A) Friedrich Nietzsche
(B) Adolf Hitler
(C) Benito Mussolini
(D) Vladimir I. Lenin
(E) Martin Heidegger

435. Which was the first twentieth-century revolutionary movement to successfully topple an existing regime?

(A) Iranian
(B) Chinese
(C) Mexican
(D) Russian
(E) French

436. Which element of the Mexican revolutionary movement of 1910 represented the greatest continuity from nineteenth-century popular movements there?

(A) Vocal demands of the Catholic church for increased power
(B) Dependence on French military assistance in order to achieve regime change
(C) Prominent role played by mestizo and Indian elements demanding land reform
(D) International acclaim for artistic representatives of the movement such as Diego Rivera
(E) Willing invitation of United States intervention to stabilize the internal situation in Mexico

437. Where in modern Europe has the rule of liberal democracy been most brief?

(A) France
(B) England
(C) Sweden
(D) Russia
(E) Germany

438. Which of the following were the main slogans the Bolsheviks put forward on their road to power in 1917?

  I. Peace
 II. Communism
III. Land
IV. Bread

(A) I, II, and IV
(B) II, III, and IV
(C) I, II, and III
(D) I, III, and IV
(E) I and IV

439. Why did the Bolshevik regime turn to a New Economic Policy in the early 1920s?

(A) A centrally planned economy was seen as the next logical step after the "War Communism" system employed during the civil war.

(B) Lenin and leading Bolshevik elements gave up socialism as a long-range goal.

(C) Lenin and leading Bolshevik elements sought to bring back free enterprise and the profit motive in order to jump-start an economy severely dislocated by World War I and the Russian Civil War.

(D) Stalin had already replaced Lenin as leader of the Bolsheviks and sought a more rapid push toward communism.

(E) Industrial development was seen as inherently exploitative of workers and was renounced in the NEP.

440. How were minority ethnic groups of the old Russian Empire treated by the new Bolshevik regime?

(A) Most individuals belonging to minorities experienced forced deportation to Siberia.

(B) Minority groups were granted semiautonomous republics bound to pursuing a socialist course.

(C) Minority ethnicities were forcibly intermarried with ethnic Russians to breed them out of existence.

(D) All minority groups were granted "Soviet Socialist Republic" territory except for Jews.

(E) Ethnic minorities were barred from membership in the Bolshevik Party.

441. Which political figure eventually emerged to lead the Bolshevik Party after the death of Lenin?

(A) Trotsky

(B) Khrushchev

(C) Gorbachev

(D) Stalin

(E) Bukharin

442. Which factor in the Russian and Chinese revolutions was not present in the French Revolution?

(A) Rural unrest
(B) Urban discontent
(C) Military intervention by neighboring or outside powers
(D) The ideas of Karl Marx and Friedrich Engels
(E) Armed struggle

443. Where in the world did the Japanese most vigorously seek to achieve territorial expansion in the years following 1914?

(A) Korea
(B) Mongolia
(C) Indonesia
(D) Pacific Islands
(E) China

444. Which development prompted Chinese nationalists and communists to suspend civil war and form a shaky common cause?

(A) Death of Sun Yat-sen
(B) Japanese invasion of China
(C) Massive American investment to build up industrial sectors in Chinese urban centers
(D) Communist long march to sanctuary in nationalist base areas in northwest China
(E) Historic summit meeting between Chiang Kai-shek and Mao Zedong

445. Which of the following statements about Western economies in the 1920s are generally accepted by historians as factors causing the Great Depression?

  I. Overproduction in industry and especially agriculture
 II. Unsustainable borrowing, lending, and stock market speculation
III. Strong government regulation of industry

(A) I and II
(B) II and III
(C) I and III
(D) II only
(E) III only

446. Which of the following answer choices places the events associated with the Great Depression in the United States in proper chronological order?

   I. Bank failures

  II. October 1929 stock market crash

 III. Skyrocketing unemployment

 IV. New Deal programs implemented by FDR

  (A) I, II, III, IV

  (B) III, I, II, IV

  (C) IV, III, II, I

  (D) II, I, III, IV

  (E) II, III, I, IV

447. Why were Great Britain and France able to insulate themselves from the Great Depression to a greater extent than Germany or the United States?

  (A) By 1929, industrial production was no longer central to their national economies.

  (B) Both nations unloaded a certain amount of surplus industrial production on markets in their extensive colonial holdings.

  (C) Strong labor movements in both countries refused to accept layoffs.

  (D) Britain and France were able to collect on loans made to Germany.

  (E) British and French parliamentary democracies took more decisive action to spur job growth than German or U.S. governments.

448. In which nation did parliamentary democracy survive the 1930s?

  (A) Spain

  (B) Germany

  (C) France

  (D) Brazil

  (E) Italy

449. Which of the following terms refers to the need and right of the German people to expand their territory according to Adolf Hitler?

  (A) *Untermenschen*

  (B) *Luftwaffe*

  (C) *Lebensraum*

  (D) *Wiener schnitzel*

  (E) *Blitzkrieg*

450. Adolf Hitler wrote which book laying out his vision and program for Germany's rise to world supremacy?

(A) *State and Revolution*
(B) *The Communist Manifesto*
(C) *Mein Kampf*
(D) *Civilization and Its Discontents*
(E) *The Great Gatsby*

451. How was the Spanish Civil War different from World War II?

(A) In the Spanish Civil War, civilian populations were subjected to aerial bombing.
(B) In the Spanish Civil War, Soviet-supplied forces fought fascist armies on European soil while liberal democracies delayed action.
(C) In the Spanish Civil War, fascists emerged victorious.
(D) In the Spanish Civil War, industrial-era weaponry was employed.
(E) In the Spanish Civil War, fighting raged in both town and countryside.

452. Which global trend had a significant impact in Latin America in the 1930s and 1940s?

  I. Slumping demand for raw materials on world markets
 II. Growing influence of fascism
III. Independence struggles in colonized regions

(A) I only
(B) I and II
(C) I and III
(D) II and III
(E) III only

453. Which policy course did Japanese and German governments take to reverse the economic difficulties of the 1930s?

(A) Stimulation of industry through war preparation
(B) Provision of social insurance through liberal democratic parliamentary means
(C) Worker control of industry
(D) Shift in orientation from industrial to agricultural production
(E) Laissez-faire approach toward economic policy

454. Which element of German fascism was NOT also found in 1930s Japan?

(A) Suspension of parliamentary authority

(B) Ideology of racial supremacy

(C) State-sanctioned mob violence against ethnic minorities

(D) Annexation of nearby territory

(E) Repression of unions

455. Which term do historians employ to describe both Hitler's Germany and Stalin's USSR?

(A) Fascist

(B) Communist

(C) Totalitarian

(D) Democratic

(E) Republican

456. Which of the following were offered by the Stalin regime as reasons to pursue collectivization of agriculture and Five-Year Plans in industry after 1928?

   I. Reversal of the NEP and inculcation of socialist habits among the Soviet masses

  II. Reduction of the Soviet population to environmentally sustainable levels

 III. Rapid industrialization to prepare for a second imperialist invasion of the USSR

(A) I only

(B) I and II

(C) II and III

(D) III only

(E) I and III

457. Which Soviet leader was a leading force in imposing economic, diplomatic, and political reforms after 1985 that contributed directly to the demise of Soviet socialism?

(A) Nikolay Bukharin

(B) Leonid Brezhnev

(C) Mikhail Gorbachev

(D) Nikita Khrushchev

(E) Lavrenty Beria

458. Which best characterizes weaknesses of the Soviet economy after World War II?
    I. Inflexible central planning
   II. Low worker morale and productivity
  III. Raw-material shortages

(A) I and II
(B) II and III
(C) I and III
(D) I only
(E) II only

459. Which Latin American nation stood apart from a general trend away from authoritarian or military rule that had taken hold across the region by the 1990s?

(A) Argentina
(B) Chile
(C) The Dominican Republic
(D) Panama
(E) Cuba

460. The growing integration of all the peoples of the planet into a single economic and political model and accelerating sharing of cultural symbols is termed

(A) Egalitarianism
(B) Simulacra
(C) Postmodernism
(D) Globalization
(E) Universalism

461. Which is the most popular and accessible method worldwide of accessing the efficiencies of a new "information economy"?

(A) Mobile phones
(B) Personal computers
(C) Local libraries
(D) Satellite television
(E) Major newspapers

462. Which is most accurate about Western economic interests overseas in the postcolonial era?
  - I. They have been imposed through formal colonization of lands and peoples of the developing world.
  - II. They are pursued by multinational corporations.
  - III. They have dwindled to the point of insignificance.

  - (A) I and II
  - (B) II and III
  - (C) I only
  - (D) II only
  - (E) III only

463. U.S. forces have seen military action most frequently to which region in the post–Cold War era?
  - (A) Pacific Rim
  - (B) Latin America
  - (C) Middle East and Central Asia
  - (D) Western Europe
  - (E) Caribbean Sea

464. What was the nationality of the majority of September 11 hijackers?
  - (A) Iraqi
  - (B) Palestinian
  - (C) Saudi Arabian
  - (D) Afghan
  - (E) Iranian

465. How are the nations of Latin America unique within the "Third World"?
  - (A) They have struggled to emerge from a dependent role in the global economy.
  - (B) They have experienced civil war in the post–WWII era.
  - (C) They gained political independence in the nineteenth century, in general.
  - (D) They continue to use a language imposed by colonial administrators in internal state affairs.
  - (E) Women have risen to high levels of political leadership.

466. Which of the following twentieth-century Latin American regimes survived CIA-supported efforts to bring them down?

    I. Arbenz regime in Guatemala

    II. Castro regime in Cuba

    III. Allende regime in Chile

    (A) I only

    (B) II only

    (C) III only

    (D) I and III

    (E) I and II

467. Which independent developing-country regime entered what is best termed as a dependent economic relationship with the Soviet Union that lasted until the collapse of the USSR in the early 1990s?

    (A) Ghana

    (B) Egypt

    (C) India

    (D) Zaire (Congo)

    (E) Cuba

468. When compared with the case of Mexico in the years since World War II, the people of Cuba have experienced greater progress in each of the following EXCEPT:

    (A) Job security

    (B) Housing

    (C) Literacy

    (D) Life expectancy

    (E) Emigration rights

469. How did local Catholic church leaders demonstrate sensitivity to demands of the poor for social justice in twentieth-century Latin America?

    (A) Demanding special infusions of charity from the Vatican that wiped out poverty in their parishes

    (B) Formulation of a "liberation theology"

    (C) Organization of sophisticated adoption schemes whereby the majority of children in poverty in Latin America were adopted by middle-class families in the West and sent to live there

    (D) Renunciation of Christianity in favor of orthodox Marxist socialism

    (E) Entering national elections, winning, and implementing land reform policies

470. Which is the most common pattern of migration in the Americas today?

(A) From North America into Latin America

(B) From Latin American countryside to Latin American cities

(C) From Latin American cities into the Latin American countryside

(D) From Latin America into North America

(E) Out of the Americas to Europe

471. Which of the following nations did not succumb to military rule in the post–WWII era?

(A) Bolivia

(B) Mexico

(C) El Salvador

(D) Argentina

(E) Venezuela

472. Which Latin American nation faced some of the first major U.S. military action overseas of the post–Cold War era?

(A) Cuba

(B) Venezuela

(C) Haiti

(D) Mexico

(E) Panama

473. The United States pursued its interests in Latin America after World War II in all of the following forms EXCEPT

(A) Direct annexation

(B) Covert action to overthrow regimes perceived to be Soviet friendly

(C) Diplomatic pressure in international organizations

(D) Peace Corps presence

(E) The IMF and World Bank

474. NAFTA has more closely integrated the economies of Canada, the United States, and

(A) Russia

(B) China

(C) Mexico

(D) Venezuela

(E) Brazil

475. Which of the following periods have been grouped together by world historians into a time called an "Age of Catastrophe" lasting from 1914 to 1945?

(A) World War I, Great Depression, Cold War
(B) Napoleonic Wars, World War I, World War II
(C) World War I, Great Depression, World War II
(D) World War II, Cold War, post–Cold War era
(E) Great Depression, World War II, Cold War

476. Which of the following trends were seen in the twentieth century?

(A) Rise and fall of communism and political independence for the former colonies
(B) Rise and fall of communism and the eradication of global poverty
(C) Eradication of global poverty and the onset of human-induced climate change
(D) Slowed population growth in industrialized regions and uninterrupted economic growth
(E) Political independence for the former colonies and uninterrupted economic growth

477. Which of the following does NOT belong in a list of major impacts of the First World War?

(A) Bolshevik Revolution in Russia
(B) Rise of the United States and Japan
(C) Birth of the League of Nations
(D) Rise of nationalist sentiment in colonized regions of the globe
(E) Independence for India

478. Where did white rule persist longest on the African continent?

(A) Rhodesia
(B) South Africa
(C) Angola
(D) Nigeria
(E) Ethiopia

479. What was the major motive behind the formation of the Triple Entente?

(A) Free trade and tariff reduction
(B) Coordinated efforts to subdue uprisings by colonized peoples
(C) Fear of Germany's growing power, especially naval power
(D) Cultural exchange
(E) Spread of Christianity

480. Which of the following is not one of the major factors historians point to as a contributing cause of World War I?

- (A) Militarism
- (B) Alliance systems
- (C) Imperialism
- (D) Nationalism
- (E) Communism

481. How did the First World War defy expectations of political elites in the West once it had begun?

- (A) The conflict was longer and bloodier than expected.
- (B) Alliance systems did not survive the war intact.
- (C) Russia turned from czarism to communism.
- (D) A and C
- (E) A, B, and C

482. Which of the following best characterizes the transfer of power associated with the decolonization process?

- (A) Elite to masses
- (B) Women to men
- (C) Religious to secular
- (D) Elite to elite
- (E) Men to women

483. Which best summarizes political trends in the West during the First World War?

- (A) Government regulation was eased as laissez-fair policy was seen as crucial to boosting wartime economic production.
- (B) Parliamentary democracy was suspended and emergency executive rule was implemented in order to facilitate rapid decision making.
- (C) Government authority increased through takeover of key industries for war production, restrictions on civil liberties, and issuance of pro-war propaganda.
- (D) Labor movements rose to power in socialist revolutions.
- (E) Political trends continued basically unchanged by wartime pressures.

484. Which of the following answer choices best explains why women won the right to vote in many Western societies after World War I?

(A) Female combat veterans returned home demanding political equality.

(B) Female nurses who cared for injured troops in the trenches won broad-based sympathy.

(C) Crucial contributions in wartime factory production lent legitimacy to ongoing calls for political and social equality.

(D) Feminist movements got their start during the First World War.

(E) Immediate granting of the right to vote to women in Soviet Russia was an embarrassment on the world stage for male-dominated liberal democracies where the movement for women's suffrage was decades old.

485. Which of the following current-day nations would have contributed troops to the Central Powers during the First World War?

(A) India

(B) Australia

(C) Czechoslovakia

(D) Russia

(E) South Africa

486. Which member of the victorious Allies emerged most dissatisfied from the Versailles settlement?

(A) Germany

(B) France

(C) United States

(D) Japan

(E) Great Britain

487. Which result of World War I did the most to spark nationalist movements in the colonized portions of the globe?

(A) Destruction of European industrial capacity in the war forced colonies toward economic independence.

(B) British and French promises for self-rule made to colonized elites during the war were broken soon thereafter.

(C) The Versailles settlement forced colonial powers to agree to timetables for colonial independence.

(D) Bolshevik-inspired revolutions broke out in the cities of the major imperialist powers.

(E) Wartime industrial production greatly increased numbers of Western women working in factories.

488. Which anticolonial struggle is recognized as establishing a template for twentieth-century independence movements that included leadership by Western-educated elites and nonviolent protest?

(A) American Revolution
(B) Haitian Revolution
(C) India's independence movement
(D) Ghana's independence movement
(E) Algeria's independence movement

489. Which colonized African region had a well-established indigenous anticolonial movement in place even before World War I?

(A) Ghana
(B) South Africa
(C) Algeria
(D) Egypt
(E) Congo

490. Which British official indicated support for the creation of a Jewish homeland in Palestine soon after World War I?

(A) Winston Churchill
(B) Theodor Herzl
(C) Neville Chamberlain
(D) Lord Balfour
(E) Margaret Thatcher

491. Which belligerent power of the First World War carried out an early exit from the hostilities and negotiated a separate peace treaty?

(A) France
(B) The United States
(C) Russia
(D) Austria-Hungary
(E) Germany

492. Which of the following had NOT experienced fascist aggression or takeover prior to World War II?

(A) Ethiopia
(B) Czechoslovakia
(C) Great Britain
(D) Spain
(E) China

493. Which of the following was an element of the fighting in World War II that remained unchanged from World War I?

(A) More rapid movement of troops in land battles through deployment of mechanized divisions

(B) Wide-ranging naval action across the Pacific Ocean

(C) Deliberate targeting of civilian populations

(D) Aerial dogfights between fighter planes

(E) Key role of amphibious operations

494. Which of the following answer choices best defines the practice of "total war"?

(A) Massive propaganda efforts to unite a population for war

(B) Government takeover of industries that are key for war production

(C) Targeting all war-fighting capacities of the enemy, including industrial and civilian targets

(D) Conscription

(E) All of the above

495. The invasion of which country led to the slowing and eventual reversal of the German blitzkrieg?

(A) France

(B) Belgium

(C) The USSR

(D) Great Britain

(E) Spain

496. Which is NOT true of the Nazi death camps?

(A) Most were located in Poland.

(B) Escape was impossible.

(C) A variety of methods were employed in carrying out executions.

(D) They were staffed by German and non-German guards.

(E) They were carefully planned and constructed.

497. Which of the following is NOT an argument put forward in debates among historians about factors contributing to President Truman's decision to employ atomic weapons against civilian populations in Japan?

(A) Prevailing racist notions in U.S. society made wiping out Asian civilian populations morally acceptable.

(B) Using atomic bombs would bring about a rapid Japanese surrender and avoid the massive U.S. casualties expected in an invasion of the Japanese homeland.

(C) Sensing a fraying alliance and potential rivalry at war settlement conferences in Yalta and Potsdam, Truman wanted to demonstrate U.S. power to the USSR in no uncertain terms.

(D) Congress was demanding tangible results from huge sums of money poured into Manhattan Project research into atomic weapons.

(E) Successful detonation of atomic weapons in battle was widely seen at the time as the first step toward the peaceful application of weapons research to nuclear energy production.

498. Which of the following legacies of British colonial rule proved most disruptive in the immediate aftermath of Indian independence?

(A) Education of diverse Indian elites in a common English language

(B) Hindu-Muslim rivalry fostered by colonial divide and rule practices

(C) Establishment of parliamentary democratic norms in government

(D) Military training provided to Indian sepoys

(E) Toleration of caste distinctions

499. How did the independence movement in colonial settler societies such as Algeria or Kenya differ from that in nonsettler societies?

(A) In nonsettler societies the independence struggle was more likely to turn violent.

(B) In settler societies constructive negotiations tended to yield power-sharing government coalitions between settlers and representatives of the indigenous populations.

(C) Nonsettler societies experienced a smooth transition to independence with steady economic growth and rising per capita incomes based on healthy industrial sectors put in place by colonial administrators.

(D) In settler societies the independence struggle was more likely to turn violent.

(E) Settler societies experienced a smooth transition to independence with steady economic growth and rising per capita incomes based on healthy industrial sectors put in place by European settlers.

500. Which event precipitated the formal creation of the state of Israel in 1947?
- (A) Multilateral U.S.-Soviet-Palestinian-Jewish negotiations
- (B) The Balfour declaration
- (C) UN-sanctioned partition of Palestine
- (D) Negotiated agreement between Zionist leaders and a unified Palestinian leadership
- (E) Arab League approval

ANSWERS

Chapter 1

1. (E) Civilization in this sense implies a level of complexity in social organization that requires a sedentary lifestyle.

2. (C) Sedentary agriculture emerges with the greatest ease in river valleys.

3. (D) Archaeologists have discovered the oldest evidence of civilization in the Tigris, Euphrates, and Nile River valleys, all of which belong to the greater Middle East region.

4. (C) The Sumerians settled into Mesopotamia (now modern Iraq). This is the earliest known civilization in the world and may also be referred to as the "cradle of civilization."

5. (D) Many portions of Hammurabi's Code make specific provisions based on the social class of the individuals involved. The passage provides no basis to make any other choice.

6. (E) No evidence supports the claim that the Chinese were involved with the building of the ancient Egyptian pyramids.

7. (D) Formidable mountain ranges and desert expanses separate the Chinese river valleys from the Middle East. However, archaeological evidence of long-distance trade connecting early Indus civilization and the Middle East has been found.

8. (C) This fact is reflected in the root of the word *phonics*, familiarity with which is key to reading.

9. (A) Writing was put to this purpose wherever it arose. Watch out for choice **(D)**; the Inca had no formal writing system but kept records by counting colored and knotted strings called *quipu*.

10. (A) *Perennial* means "growing once a year." Watch out for choice **(C)**; Mesoamerican civilization had no domesticated draft animals. Draft animals provide muscle power and include oxen, cows, and horses.

11. (A) Since Christianity and Islam are derived from Judaism, this makes Abraham an important historical figure to study.

12. (B) This characteristic is more widely recognized by Westerners in Confucian and Hindu traditions than in the Christian tradition. Numerous biblical passages exhort the poor and the slave to accept their lots in life and obey their masters. Choice **(A)** is false regarding Confucianism while choice **(E)** is true for Christianity only.

13. (B) Nile, Yellow, and Tigris-Euphrates valleys respectively; **(A)** is false for Shang China while choices **(C)**, **(D)**, and **(E)** are false for all three civilizations.

14. (C) Recreational use of gunpowder dates from the Song Dynasty (tenth to thirteenth centuries CE, roughly) with military application coming thereafter.

15. (A) Keep in mind the importance of the Greek navy in its rise to regional power.

16. (C) While monarchs before may have been limited by custom, historians date the emergence of constitutional monarchy to the British Isles in the centuries following the signing of the Magna Carta in the early thirteenth century.

17. (A) While the first and third bullet points are true for the Maya, the second one is not, making Harappan the only possible choice.

18. (A) The other civilizations on the list succumbed to human-induced shocks of war or peasant revolt. Less evidence for this persists to draw the same conclusion about the Indus River valley civilization.

19. (A) *Cultural diffusion* means "the spread of ideas or practices from one region to another," and this was evident with the Roman elite and their taste for silk garments.

20. (D) Construction of ships from metal required industrial techniques not developed until the nineteenth century when blast furnaces and the Bessemer process for creating steel were developed. Before the Industrial Revolution metalwork was limited to projects or items that could be produced by hand by a blacksmith.

21. (D) One of the great unsolved mysteries of the ancient world is that Harappan writing has not yet been deciphered.

22. (D) Cuneiform emerged in the Sumerian civilization. A pictograph is a simplified visual representation of an object in written form, an ideograph is a symbol that represents a concept, and phonetic symbols represent sounds. Cuneiform was a pictographic writing system.

23. (A) Archaeological excavation at all four sites reveal the earliest traces of monumental building, writing tablets, and urban living in the Tigris-Euphrates valley, where Sumerian civilization was born.

24. (E) Archaeological findings indicate that agriculture emerged roughly ten thousand years ago—long after *Homo erectus* had gone extinct by all available data.

25. (B) *Revolution* is a term applied to any abrupt shift in a course of human events that was sparked in a specific location or region. This question asks us to consider time frame. Political revolutions, such as the French or Russian revolution, tend to unfold more quickly, while nonpolitical revolutions (scientific, industrial) take place over a period of decades. Only the transition to sedentary agriculture took place over a period of centuries or even millennia.

26. (C) Paleolithic peoples had domesticated the wolf long before any "farm" animal. Choices **(A)**, **(D)**, and **(E)** represent practices that died out, while choice **(B)** is not true of Paleolithic peoples.

27. (D) Sedentary society tended to give rise to social stratification, including slavery.

28. (B) Pastoral nomads established the viability of herding of animals as an economic activity; this viability continued through history until today. Take note that choice **(E)** is inaccurate.

29. (E) The "New World" refers to the Americas and the Western Hemisphere. Maize was an early crop that was unique to these civilizations.

30. (C) Large numbers of small children lessen the mobility of preagricultural nomadic groups; additionally, increased food output of agricultural production provided a basis for greater confinement of women of child-bearing age to the home.

31. (A) Biological and archaeological evidence supports this choice and none of the others.

32. (E) This is the basic model of early labor specialization. For choice **(C)**, archaeological digs of Paleolithic-era sites have revealed the presence of stone tools far from quarry locations, indicating long-distance trade was practiced. Choices **(A)**, **(B)**, and **(D)** are false.

33. (B) Ailments such as chicken pox, swine flu, and bird flu in their very names indicate the propensity for pathogen sharing between people and domesticated animals. It also took awhile for plumbing to be invented. Sedentary peoples settled next to their pathogen-producing waste as well. Nomadic people never had to deal with these health hazards as they moved away from their wastes. All other choices are false.

34. (E) Genetic research supports the origin of anatomically modern humans in Africa, only.

35. (B) To some extent these three developments occurred simultaneously, but to the extent that one is a precondition for the next, this choice lays them out in correct order.

36. (D) Slash and burn requires the least manipulation of the natural world. Anthropological studies indicate that it is practiced by populations in a transitional phase between nomadic and agricultural practices.

37. (B) Radiocarbon dating of human remains, rock paintings (Australia in particular), and genetic studies all support this choice.

38. (D) Australian aborigines maintained a hunter-gatherer lifestyle until the continent was colonized by Westerners.

39. (E) *Neolithic* means "new stone age" and *paleolithic* means "old stone age." Neolithic has also become shorthand for "settled agricultural" and while some settled agriculturalists developed metal, preagricultural peoples generally did not for anything more than ornamental purposes.

40. (B) Hellas was the ancient name for Greece. *Hellenistic*, therefore, means "Greek-like" and dates from the spread of Greek culture along with the armies of Alexander, the greatest Greek empire builder.

41. (E) The rapid conquests of Alexander's armies fostered a Greek-directed sharing of ideas from the Indus River valley across the Middle East to the Mediterranean basin.

42. (E) This practice never changed; **(A)** and **(C)** were discontinued, and **(B)** and **(D)** never happened in any way that survives in the historical record.

43. (B) Based on fragmentary evidence, important reforms that lay the basis for Greek democracy date to the period of Solon's rule. Choices **(A)**, **(C)**, and **(D)** were philosophers while choice **(E)** was a playwright.

44. (E) Athenian women experienced a highly cloistered lifestyle even in relation to other women in the ancient world.

45. (A) The Silk Roads connected these two civilizations. Scandinavia was more or less uncivilized while Polynesian and Olmec peoples were isolated by vast oceans. Gupta civilization had yet to exist in the days of classical Greek rule.

46. (D) Herodotus, sometimes called the "father of history," is not part of the chain of teaching that flowed from Socrates to Plato to Aristotle to Alexander.

47. (C) is accurate for both empires. Choices **(A)**, **(D)**, and **(E)** are true for neither. Choice **(B)** was true for Han but not Roman civilization.

48. (B) A social hierarchy was common to all three and is also key to state formation.

49. (C) Monastic life refers to life in a monastery or, in this case, a nunnery. Monasticism represented one of the few exits for women from the generally restrictive gender roles of family life of the classical and postclassical worlds.

50. (D) Asoka moved the Maurya Empire toward Buddhism; Constantine's conversion moved Rome toward Christianity (and had more of a lasting impact in European civilization than Asoka's conversion did in India).

51. (E) Roman imperial rule depended on a combination of military occupation and local assistance.

52. (D) Nomads frequently served to communicate ideas and trends from one distant civilization to another. This helped to foster trade between civilizations.

53. (B) The proximity to older centers of civilization helped the Eastern Roman world during the breakdown of the Roman imperial unity.

54. (C) The Roman Empire formed a near complete rim around the Mediterranean, the richest region under Roman control.

55. (A) The "overexpansion" of the Roman Empire is a well-studied phenomenon and is intimately connected with dependence on unreliable hired mercenaries to represent Roman authority in far-flung regions.

56. (C) As indicated in question 53, this is a matter of factual knowledge that one needs to become familiar with.

57. (B) The concepts of citizenship (as opposed to subject status) or elected representation of nonaristocratic elements in government was underdeveloped to nonexistent in the civilizations listed other than the Roman civilization.

58. (E) Referring to question 44, choice **(E)** is most true even taking into consideration variations across city-states.

59. (C) Referring to question 11, the Old Testament of the Bible is derived from Jewish holy texts.

60. (E) The Ziggurats were massive monuments built during Sumerian and Mesopotamian times; Doric, Ionic, and Corinthian are all styles associated with columns, and the Parthenon is the most famous classical Greek structure to survive into the modern era.

61. (C) The Persian Empire was the largest empire in the ancient world until the days of Alexander, and it was the first to encompass land in Asia, Africa, and Europe. It was the European ambitions of Persian imperial power and also its time frame, 550 to 330 BCE, that made this empire a constant threat to Greek independence.

62. (A) The bullets form a useful reminder of key features of Indian geography—especially the mention of monsoon weather patterns!

63. (D) Tension between regional autonomy and central authority is an abiding theme in the history of the Indian subcontinent.

64. (B) The Hindu tradition and caste system are trademarks of early Indian culture, while the other choices contain a grain of truth at best.

65. (B) Buddhism, Christianity, Judaism, and Islam all trace their origins to the teachings of a central or founding figure. Hinduism stands apart with its absence of a prophetic founding figure; its central tenets were compiled over centuries and collected in holy texts such as the Vedas.

66. (E) Hinduism relies on texts, the Vedas being key, as a founding impulse, not the revelatory experiences of a prophetic or divine individual like the others listed in choices **(A)** through **(D)**.

67. (A) Rejection of caste is Buddhism's signal break with Hindu tradition.

68. (A) Dharma teaches acceptance of one's caste and role as key to spiritual peace and blessing.

69. (B) *The Analects* are a collection of Confucius's writings. Confucianism is not a spiritual faith but is closer to a political philosophy.

70. (C) The concept of zero is most associated with the Gupta Empire, a fact that one needs to become familiar with.

71. (E) Buddhists carried over the belief in reincarnation from Hinduism.

72. (C) Later empires to rule India, such as the Mughal (and even the British), confronted the same challenge. Recognizing long-term patterns like these are crucial for success in this advanced placement course.

73. (A) The classical period, lasting roughly from 1000 BCE to 600 CE, saw state and imperial structures grow to become quite refined and stable after millennia of evolution in the major centers of civilization. Stable imperial authority was the key to long-distance trade.

74. (E) Reviewing questions 67 and 71, Buddhism is viewed as a modification of Hinduism.

75. (B) Buddhism generally spread north and east but not much farther west than Persia or Central Asia, ruling out Buddhist presence in Mesopotamia.

76. (D) Reflective of the generally decentralized nature of the Hindu faith, castes have developed on an occupational and village-by-village basis, making thousands the best choice.

77. (A) The Koran is Arabic in origin while the Vedas and Bhagavad Gita have backgrounds from India.

78. (B) Choices **(C)** and **(D)** can be eliminated immediately. Looking at the remaining, China maintained generally superior craftsmanship and manufacturing capacity until the Industrial Revolution after the year 1800.

79. (E) Legalism prescribes harsh punishment to achieve order, unlike Confucianism, which relies on filial obligation and was the guiding philosophy of the Qin dynasty that unified China for the first time. Confucianism was not established as the guiding philosophy of a unified central imperial state until the Han dynasty, one dynasty after the Qin.

80. (A) Legalism states that humans need to be controlled using laws to maintain order. Referring to the previous question, this is not part of Confucianism.

81. (D) Confucianism did not take root as state ideology until the Han dynasty.

82. (B) Shi Huangdi followed legalism while some early Tang leaders, such as Empress Wu, were influenced significantly by Buddhism.

83. (A) Choice **(A)** is the best description of Confucianism. Choice **(B)** would match most forms of religious fundamentalism, **(C)** would match any religion with an afterlife, **(D)** fits the bill for various strains of Marxism and anarchism, and **(E)** fits Daoism more closely.

84. (D) The pervasive nature of Chinese patriarchy singles out this choice as the false one. As with many civilizations, women would have difficulty climbing the socioeconomic ladder for some time to come.

85. (A) Ethnocentrism means, roughly, preference for one's own kind, and this choice summarizes a recurrent theme in the history of dynastic China.

86. (E) According to Confucius, everyone had a specific role in society and, with that role, certain duties to complete. This would make it clear to all people as to what was expected of them so that order could be maintained.

87. (E) For centuries before the modern times China was a male-dominated society. Knowing this, the mere presence of statement II invalidates all other choices.

88. (E) Buddhism came from India. The remaining choices are Chinese in origin.

89. (E) This is the crucial difference to keep in mind; all of the other choices are more true for Hinduism. Choice **(A)** is incorrect because both belief systems uphold patriarchal gender roles.

90. (C) All of the major civilizations that historians label "classical" date roughly from the period 1000 BCE to 600 CE and featured strong state structures able to impose order and stability. This political stability helped form the basis for cultural flowering, economic growth, and robust trade. Maurya, Gupta, Greek, Roman, and Han civilizations fit this description.

91. (D) Becoming a dynasty generally requires military acumen outside the range of expertise of the typical Confucian scholar-bureaucrat. Statement I fits Han and Tang origins. Statement II is true for Sui and Song eras, while statement III matches Yuan and Qing dynasties. IV is not accurate for any Chinese dynasty.

92. (A) This crucial distinction explains an Eastern preeminence over the West in economic and political organization that was to last through the feudal and far into the early modern eras.

93. (C) The Mandate of Heaven focuses on the conduct of the ruler. It helps to avoid abuse by the ruler and calls for only the best ruler to serve in the position.

94. (B) This period of decentralized rule cried out for a thinker who would formulate a framework for the return and maintenance of social order. It is unsurprising Confucius hails from this period.

95. (B) This statement holds true for every rising or new dynasty and is a very useful pattern to keep in mind. Choice **(C)** was inaccurate for all dynasties except the Yuan. Choice **(E)** was true for the Han but not for the Qin. Choice **(D)** was true for neither, while choice **(A)** was true for the Han and not the Qin.

96. (B) Daoism has a focus on harmony with nature and an orientation toward natural as opposed to human affairs as key to a fulfilled life.

97. (A) Refer to question #89. Once again, traditional Chinese patriarchy helps us to find an incorrect statement.

98. (C) The harmony and balance of Daoism is represented most widely in the Western mind by the yin-yang symbol.

99. (D) Keep in mind that a Daoist is relatively detached or unconcerned with political or economic concerns that require a lust for power or wealth.

100. (B) Bronze, jade, and silk were all manipulated by the Chinese with intricate detail. Choices **(A)** and **(D)** are more associated with Mediterranean civilizations. Choice **(E)** is unlikely as the arts were generally financed by and represent the elites. Keep in mind that classical Chinese art in particular tends to depict natural scenes and de-emphasize humans.

Chapter 2

101. (E) The Mongol expansion stopped in Eastern Europe, in what constitutes present-day Romania.

102. (D) Silk Roads passed through the Central Asian heartlands of the Mongol Empire.

103. (C) This merit system helped to explain the consistently superior quality of Mongol military forces. Nomadic people, not possessing property in land, are generally less inculcated with a respect for inherited wealth and lineage.

104. (C) The phalanx infantry formation was a Greek military technique where the soldiers aligned in a massive rectangular formation.

105. **(B)** Kiev was ravaged by the Mongols in late 1240. Kiev never recovered its preeminent status in Russian civilization.

106. **(C)** Mesopotamia in general, and Baghdad in particular, represented the economic and administrative heart of the Islamic world. Choices **(B), (D),** and **(E)** occurred outside the time frame of Abbasid rule, and the Crusades never represented a mortal threat to Islamic civilization.

107. **(A)** Kublai Khan ruled from the imperial center at Beijing, though he had traditional Mongol-style tents (or yurts) placed in the Forbidden City just to show who was boss!

108. **(C)** Mongols were more appreciative of trade as a source of taxation, as well as new ideas from other civilizations, than were traditional Chinese elites.

109. **(C)** After the death of Genghis Khan the Mongol Empire was split into a number of khanates. These root-word games may seem trivial now but are important later on in the course, since across the globe nationhood winds up replacing all manner of monarchy and aristocratic rule. *Kingdom, principality, empire,* and *county* are of similar derivation.

110. **(D)** Known in the West as Tamerlane, Timur-I Lang's brief fourteenth-century expansion reached Persia, the Fertile Crescent, India, and southern Russia.

111. **(E)** Mongol contact with Chinese civilization made the Mongols a conduit for gunpowder to the West.

112. **(A)** Integration of west, central, eastern, and southern Africa into world trade was achieved via Muslim contact as well as trans-Saharan and Indian Ocean trade networks.

113. **(D)** Refer to the explanation in question 112. The Sahara Desert lies in the northern third of the African continent.

114. **(C)** State structures arise in part to reinforce class division, protect elites, and suppress slave uprisings. The archaeological, anthropological, and historical records do not show endemic class conflict to be a feature of stateless societies.

115. **(C)** Choice **(A)** is accurate for some but not all of postclassical black Africa. Choices **(B), (D),** and **(E)** are not accurate descriptors of the same.

116. **(A)** Coptic Christianity's reach was limited roughly to Ethiopia. The other choices had little to no presence whatsoever.

117. **(D)** Muslim rule spread out of Arabia, across North Africa, and around the Strait of Gibraltar into the Iberian Peninsula in the seventh and eighth centuries CE. None of the other choices adjoin North Africa.

118. **(C)** Egypt's position at the northeast corner of the African continent near the isthmus of Suez has made it a crucial entry point into Africa since the dawn of civilization.

119. (C) The Bedouin, while many converted, are an Arabian ethnic group. The Berbers are a North African group exposed very early to Islam. The Ethiopians remained Christian, and the South African Khoisan and Zulu remained (more or less) unconverted to Islam.

120. (A) Coptic Christianity has been a mass faith in these societies from the days of the Roman Empire up until the present. Refer to question 116.

121. (D) Sudanic states spanned the Sahel band of grassland where the southern Sahara Desert transitions into the savanna and tropical climates of central Africa. Congo (sometimes spelled Kongo and called Zaire in the mid- to late twentieth century) is a central African society based around the Congo River, the second longest river in Africa.

122. (D) This is a popular question on world history exams. Levels of planning and organization required to carry out this trade rivaled those associated with early Atlantic crossings of Columbus and others.

123. (D) More commonly known as Mansa Musa; an easy mnemonic device (MMM) is used to associate him with the correct West African kingdom of the postclassical era—Mali (Mansa Musa from Mali).

124. (B) In the early postclassical era Western Europe (cities A, C, and D) was slowly regenerating centralized political authority and long-distance trade, while literacy and urbanization was just beginning to penetrate Russia (city E). In the same period, roughly 600 to 1000, West Africa was a center of all three.

125. (E) Take note that these three important West African kingdoms of the postclassical era have a chronological order that matches their alphabetical order.

126. (C) Devout Muslims did not practice ancestor worship but did relax female dress codes that were growing stricter in the rest of Islamic civilization at the time. This process of religious adaptation is an example of syncretism, or adjustment and combination of ideas.

127. (C) Swahili dates from the expansion of Islam into sub-Saharan Africa and is spoken across a vast expanse of territory. Arabic and Bantu are the two largest linguistic groups among the choices, with Yoruba and Berber being more localized tongues.

128. (B) The Swahili coast formed the western rim of the Indian Ocean trade network, where goods of the Middle East, South Asia, and East Asia were all available.

129. (C) Timbuktu is an important postclassical West African city. While some of the other choices may be a bit obscure, you should be sure that Timbuktu was NOT on the East African coast.

130. (D) Ivory is taken mainly from elephant tusks and has been worked by artisans from many civilizations—including African ones. The other listed materials are more associated with Mediterranean civilization (marble, oil paint, mosaic tile) or China (jade).

131. (B) In sub-Saharan Africa a higher proportion of elite individuals converted to Islam, perhaps due to closer contact with Muslim merchants, than did persons of lower social status.

132. (E) In no region listed did a majority convert to Islam, with the possible exception of Indonesia.

133. (D) Lack of a clear succession principle has been a lasting source of conflict in the religion and politics of Islamic civilization.

134. (C) Islamic civilization at its height encompassed more territory than the others listed. Keep in mind that Mongol power never penetrated Africa.

135. (A) The Bedouin people who populated the Arabian peninsula prior to the rise of Islam fall into the category of pastoral nomadic.

136. (D) Muhammad's retreat to Medina and his triumphant return to Mecca are seminal events in the early spread of the Islamic faith.

137. (C) Baghdad was the center of the Abbasid caliphate, and Istanbul became the capital of the Ottoman Empire.

138. (C) Khadija, daughter of Khuwaylid, was the wealthy widow of a prominent merchant.

139. (E) The other choices translate, roughly, as follows: *hijab*—clothing that preserves female modesty; *hajj*—pilgrimage to Mecca; *hadith*—the sayings and actions of Muhammad not contained in the Koran; *zakat*—alms giving.

140. (C) These are the only two that shared space and time with the expanding Umayyad caliphate.

141. (A) The Indus River valley of northwest India had been a target of imperial conquest from the days of Alexander, and Spain and Morocco was the farthest westward outpost of the old Roman Mediterranean imperium. Islam at its height guided the trade and collected the knowledge of this vast, rich, and ancient zone of civilized humanity.

142. (D) *Dhimmi* translates roughly to "people of the book," which takes in the Abrahamic faiths and even Hinduism, but not animism, which was dismissed as paganism.

143. (C) Women were not allowed to have multiple spouses. The other choices form a decent summary of rights women had.

144. (B) In comparison with contemporary civilizations, women in the Islamic world experienced the greatest latitude in both the private and public spheres.

145. (C) The Umayyad caliphate (680–750) achieved the initial expansion of Islamic power in the decades and centuries after the death of Muhammad. The longer-lasting Abbasid caliphate (750–1258) oversaw a consolidation of Islamic power, continuing until it was toppled by Mongol invasions in the mid-thirteenth century.

146. (D) As a nice round number, you can keep in mind that in about the year 1000 CE Baghdad was perhaps the most sophisticated city on the planet. Only Chinese urban centers would have rivaled it.

147. (E) This serves as a useful summary of areas that flowered in what historians consider an Islamic golden age. Abbasid openness to conversion of non-Arabs to Islam (less true in the Umayyad period) fostered a period of vibrant cultural and intellectual exchange.

148. (E) Founding state religion of the Roman Empire did not survive the empire's decline as state religion while Islam survived the decline of the Abbasid caliphate and remained the dominant belief system in the Middle East even after the collapse of the caliphate. While in decline, the Abbasid rulers did not convert to a new religion.

149. (A) In more Eurocentric terms, Anatolia has been termed the "Near East," as distinct from the "Middle East" surrounding the Fertile Crescent or the "Far East" that generally refers to China and Japan.

150. (D) European military outposts lasted several centuries at most. Jerusalem has never been a Christian town, and Islam split into the Sunni and Shia branches in the seventh century (the Crusades were mainly a twelfth-century phenomenon).

151. (B) While complex sedentary social organization was emerging or established in all of the other choices, none of them rivaled Chinese or Islamic levels of sophistication.

152. (A) Mass conversion of South Asians to Islam would have to wait until the period of the Delhi Sultanate and the Mughal Empire, beginning in the thirteenth century. Anatolia, Egypt, and Morocco all saw considerable conversion rates. China never fell under Muslim control.

153. (D) Steam power is quintessentially modern and can be traced to eighteenth-century Great Britain. All postclassical civilizations qualify as premodern.

154. (E) The Slavic people were influenced by Byzantium. Take note that all of the regions listed in the question are Slavic regions.

155. (E) The eastern Mediterranean had been predominantly culturally Greek from the classical era and remained so until the arrival of the Ottoman Turks in the fifteenth century CE. The reversion from Latin back to Greek in both church and state affairs after the fall of the Western Roman Empire is evidence of this tendency.

156. (A) Neither Scandinavia, India, nor sub-Saharan Africa is adjacent to the choke point between the Black and Mediterranean seas that made Byzantium such a key trade hub in the ancient world.

157. (C) The Justinian code established a lasting legal framework, Byzantine bureaucracy is famously complex, and the Hagia Sophia was a monument to architectural grandeur. All date from the period of Justinian's rule. Diocletian launched a series of reforms that slowed, but did not reverse, the decline of the Western Roman Empire. Constantine is known for adopting Christianity as the state religion of the Roman Empire, Osman was the founding sultan of the Ottoman Empire, and Muhammad was the founder of the Muslim faith.

158. (E) Byzantine power was influential abroad, as toward the north in Russia. However, military conquest and formal annexation of territory was not a Byzantine strong suit.

159. (B) Early Russian civilization is known as "Kievan Rus."

160. (C) Refer to question 105. Lasting from the 880s to the 1240s, Kievan Rus represents an early example of the slow trend toward centralization of political power and territorial expansion that characterized trends in European monarchy in later centuries.

161. (B) In a time of collapsed authority, banditry, and relative chaos following the failure of a Confucian state (the Han), Buddhism's orientation away from earthly troubles and toward a better hereafter attracted followers. Many of them lived on or near increasingly influential monasteries.

162. (C) This is a neat bit of dynastic trivia that will gain relevance again in twentieth and twenty-first century relations between the Chinese central government and the Tibet and Xinjiang regions that were first brought under Chinese rule during the Tang era.

163. (D) Prominent families, through test preparation of their children for civil service exams or bribery, tended to remain ensconced in positions of power in the Chinese bureaucracy; other choices may have been true in rare cases but do not rise to the level of being the "best" choice to answer this question.

164. (E) Punitive measures by Tang emperors, such as confiscation of monastic lands that had gone untaxed, reduced but did not eliminate Buddhist influence.

165. (B) Neo-Confucianism dates from the Song era and attempted to merge certain basic elements of Confucianism, Daoism, and Buddhism.

166. (E) Occupying the highest mountain plateau in the world, Tibetans have kept pretty much to themselves in world history; Jurchens, Turks, and Mongols are all central Asian nomadic groups, while the Manchu hail from Manchuria.

167. (D) The Grand Canal connects the Yangtze and the Yellow river valleys, China's two most densely populated regions. Connecting the two was an important step forward in the process of Chinese unification.

168. (A) Arranged marriage and concubinage are also traditional and predate the Song era. Divorce rights and the one-child policy date from the communist era.

169. (E) China generated perhaps the largest share of key inventions of the premodern era. The rise of the Industrial Revolution in the West changed all that. Steam power dates from eighteenth-century England.

170. (D) Specifically, the Jinshi was a group composed of individuals who placed highest in the imperial examinations given every three years from the Sui dynasty of the early seventh century all the way down to 1905, when the examination system was abolished (with the exception only of a period during the Yuan dynasty when exams were suspended for a time).

171. (C) This choice is going to be incorrect about every Chinese society up until 1949, with the brief exception of the Taiping Rebellion of the 1860s.

172. (C) Areas of Japanese state formation and society listed in the other choices mirrored Chinese patterns more closely.

173. (D) Chinese naval capacity had not yet reached the level of sophistication to enable blue-water (distant from coastline) explorations necessary to meet Polynesian peoples in the Tang-Song era.

174. (B) Written in approximately 1008 CE, Lady Murasaki's *Tale of Genji* captures the pomp and circumstance of court life in the Heian era of Japanese history.

175. (C) The main trend in the postclassical era was for societies to move from a slave-based economic and social structure to one we call feudal. The similarities between European and Japanese feudalism stem in part from the relative isolation from global trade routes (as compared to the Byzantine or Islamic civilizations at the time) and the resultant necessity to base economic activity around cultivation of the land both civilizations shared.

176. (D) "High Middle Ages" refers to a period from about 1000 to 1300 and connotes something of a recovery from the Dark Ages that followed the fall of Rome in the fifth century. **(A)** and **(E)** predate the High Middle Ages, while **(B)** and **(C)** occurred after.

177. (D) Absorbed into the Muslim world, much of Spain did not experience a collapse in central authority to the same degree as the other regions listed.

178. (C) Even European ruling elites tended to be illiterate in the first centuries after the fall of Rome. Peasant illiteracy is not as surprising perhaps. Monasteries were outposts of reading and writing in this period.

179. (D) Serfdom was the dominant form of labor during the Middle Ages, replacing the slave labor that, especially in the Western Roman Empire, had become central to economic activity.

180. (C) While its organizational capacity was not military and, thus, not strictly imperial, the Catholic church was nonetheless the greatest unifying influence in the West at the time. The Holy Roman Empire did not exist yet, and Carolingian rule was limited more or less to what we now call France. Islam was limited to the Iberian Peninsula, while the Mongols had yet to emerge.

181. (A) Aristocratic checks on royal power, codified in the Magna Carta of the thirteenth-century British Isles, set a precedent for the future diminution of the power of monarchs we associate with the rise of modern democracy.

182. (E) This choice becomes accurate only in the late nineteenth century; the others are accurate in the period 600–1450.

183. (C) Scholasticism was an important step in the return of the rational tradition in Western intellectual history (which can be traced back to Aristotle) in the midst of a more general period where religious faith was dominant.

184. (D) While sea trade occurred in all the other listed choices, the center of gravity of world maritime trade in the postclassical era was an area extending from the South China Sea through Indonesia to the Indian Ocean basin.

185. (E) The answer is most likely going to have a Latin title because a saint is likely a Catholic church figure and Latin was the language of the Catholic church. Hence, a church figure in the Middle Ages most likely wrote in Latin.

186. (C) Guilds have been described as medieval precursors of labor unions. While the analogy is far from perfect, the mental connection with an organization of laborers is a useful one.

187. (C) Becoming a nun was an important exception to a more common existence within strictly defined gender roles during this time period.

188. (C) This protracted conflict had the broad effect of strengthening monarchy in ways that would be replicated and magnified in the period 1450–1750. It should also be noted that Joan of Arc was a figure in this war.

189. (C) Any contact between Native American and "Old World" civilizations that may have transpired in the period 600–1450 was of too inconsistent and insubstantial a nature to survive in the historical record.

190. (A) The Aztec civilization centered around a semitropical Valley of Mexico with irrigated lake-based agriculture, while Inca civilization radiated out from mountain highland climatic zones and made use of terrace farming, making statement III false. Statements I and II are true of both.

191. (C) No large mammals appropriate for domestication existed in the "New World," and Native American civilizations achieved remarkable degrees of architectural achievement considering that human muscle power was their sole source of power.

192. (B) The Aztec capital was built amid *chinampas*—massive landfill and floating island networks laid into Lake Texcoco in the Valley of Mexico and used for agriculture—which afforded the Aztec civilization rich soil, ease of transport, and defense in case of invasion.

193. (E) Raids by Aztec military forces into surrounding populations to capture prisoners of war for use in sacrificial ceremonies sowed seeds of resentment that Cortez was able to exploit to gain indigenous allies in his campaign against Tenochtitlan between 1519 and 1521.

194. (D) A well-organized merchant class, the *pochteca*, specialized in long-distance luxury item trade and was central to the economic activity at the Tlatelolco market; in China the merchant class was crucial to trade but was not afforded similar social status in the Confucian-dominated worldview prevalent there.

195. (C) These *calpulli* are analogous to our current-day organization of towns into neighborhoods, boroughs, or precincts where related individuals lived.

196. (B) For the Inca the sun was the chief deity, and the ruler (the "Inca") was the sun god's representative on earth, ruling with his favor and embodying his authority. This is closely related to the long-held Chinese concept of the Mandate of Heaven and the Western European concept of the divine right of kings that would develop in the early modern period.

197. (D) The Mongol Empire dominated the Silk Roads but did not establish them, and the Aztecs are more famous for their waterborne transport networks surrounding Tenochtitlan; both the Romans and the Inca made construction and maintenance of road networks central to economic and military activity in their empires.

198. (E) Cuzco, the heart of the Inca imperial administration, became the capital of Spanish-dominated Peru and continues, like Mexico City, as a once-prominent city from the pre-Columbian era upon whose location colonial and modern urban settlement has flourished.

199. (A) Inca civilization encompassed lands that extended from modern-day Colombia down the Pacific coast through Peru into Chile and inland to parts of Argentina and Bolivia.

200. (E) Aztec civilization of Mesoamerica may have reached a population of as high as twenty million according to current estimates and was the most densely populated region of the New World, surpassing Inca and other centers of human settlement.

Chapter 3

201. **(E)** European firearms were superior to African weapons and highly sought after by Africans themselves.

202. **(C)** Portuguese sailors were the first Europeans to venture down the West African coastline, starting in the early fifteenth century. They were in the best position to set up slave-trading posts (called factories) after the discovery of the New World. The shift to plantation agriculture there sent demands for slave labor skyrocketing.

203. **(D)** Roughly speaking, the sixteenth century was spent plundering the New World while the seventeenth was spent carving plantations out of the wilderness. The plantation economy was booming in the eighteenth century, and by the nineteenth century industrialization and wage labor was the most profitable investment for capital.

204. **(B)** Coastal kingdoms participated in what historians term a "gun and slave cycle," in which they traded individuals captured inland for guns and then employed those weapons in the capture of more people, pressing farther and farther inland.

205. **(D)** Northeast Africa is much closer to the Arab and Indian zones of the world economy than the Atlantic world. As for the other choices, ivory, gold, and domestic slaves were in demand around the Indian Ocean basin, and this trade was carried out by Muslim merchants who would have been the buyers of imported copies of the Koran.

206. **(C)** These Dutchmen came to be known as Boers (Dutch for "farmers"). Their descendants have been in South Africa for longer than most persons of European descent living in North America can claim to have been living here.

207. **(C)** These conflicts at first caused migrations of Boers away from coastal areas to the interior (the "Great Trek") and later bubbled over into the Boer War circa 1900.

208. **(B)** The estimated mortality rate was 30 percent on African soil and 10 percent at sea. Tales, poems, and paintings of sharks following slave ships across the oceans serve as a constant reminder of the horrors of dead or dying people being thrown overboard.

209. **(D)** Sugar cultivation on the Caribbean Islands, including Haiti, Jamaica, and Barbados, involved notoriously high mortality rates. No significant slave trade to Argentina ever developed. The tobacco, rice, and later, cotton that were cultivated in the temperate climate of the southern thirteen colonies allowed for a natural increase of the population of enslaved Africans. This is one reason why the black population of the United States continued to grow even after the Atlantic slave trade was outlawed in 1808. In fact, an internal slave trade from the older tidewater plantation areas of Maryland and Virginia down to the expanding cotton belt across Georgia, Alabama, Mississippi, Louisiana, and Texas developed after 1808.

210. (B) Slavery lasted in Brazil until 1888; it was declared illegal in Mexico in 1810, in Haiti in 1804, in the United States in 1865, and in Cuba in 1886.

211. (B) While the sugar plantations of the Caribbean Island, taken together, made up the main destination of enslaved Africans, the sugar plantations of Brazil's Atlantic coast attracted more slave ships than any other single colony on its own. The British thirteen colonies were never a major destination in the slave trade compared with points farther south.

212. (B) England was the first of these choices to ban slave trade. This began in 1808.

213. (A) The Atlantic slave trade grew during the Enlightenment era and flew in the face of concepts of natural rights belonging to all humans.

214. (C) While Russian monarchy was the largest contiguous land empire in history, one must keep in mind that much of it was relatively empty Siberian land.

215. (D) Referring to the previous question, the lands to the east of the Ural Mountains that were gained were vast and sparsely populated.

216. (D) Remember that St. Petersburg (Peter's town) is to the *west* of Moscow, a reminder of Peter the Great's general policy course.

217. (A) Serfdom was so woven into the fabric of Russian life that it was applied to the new factory system when it arrived.

218. (C) Monarchs, in general, were searching for paths to increased royal authority in the period after 1450. For Russia, westernization would serve that purpose.

219. (A) Russian eastward ambition stretched through Siberia, across the Bering Strait, and into Alaska. The United States approved the purchase of Alaska from the Russians in 1867. This event is often referred to as Seward's folly or Seward's icebox.

220. (D) Regarding world trade, Russia played to its own strengths, supplying resources that its vast territory could produce in bulk.

221. (E) Russian expansion has tended to be land based and not naval throughout the course of its history.

222. (A) No European monarch with a sense of pride wanted to fall too far behind in military capacity. We can rule out choice **(D)** if we refer to question 221.

223. (C) The early settlers of Massachusetts, the Puritans, were British citizens seeking greater religious freedom. We have no similar phenomenon in the settlement of Spanish Latin America, perhaps because religious minorities were effectively eliminated in a series of campaigns in Spain spanning from the Reconquista of 1492 when Jews and Muslims were expelled from Spain into the period of the Inquisition of the sixteenth and seventeenth centuries where Catholic orthodoxy was imposed by force on the population.

224. (C) This was particularly true in British North America.

225. (A) Terms like "mestizo" or "mulatto" arose in Spanish Latin America to reflect the commonplace racial mixing that took place there. Skin color affected social status in both locations, however.

226. (B) This can be explained in large part by the near complete disappearance of the indigenous population of the New World in the face of smallpox and war.

227. (C) These estates were called *encomiendas* and were crucial to the establishment of an agricultural economy in the Spanish New World. "Bourbon reforms" were enacted to tighten royal control as the *encomiendas* began to form power bases to challenge the rule of the Spanish monarchy in the seventeenth and eighteenth centuries.

228. (C) Columbus landed on Hispanola (which today contains the nations of Haiti and the Dominican Republic), abducted several indigenous Arawak/Carib native individuals, and returned to Spain. On subsequent voyages to the Caribbean, he set about the business of enslaving indigenous populations and setting them to work searching for gold.

229. (E) The choices above serve as a useful list to help remind us of the nuts and bolts of the move from "plunder to plantation."

230. (C) By the time sugar had supplanted silver as the New World's most valuable product, the Spanish monarchy had been displaced from key sugar-producing locations (the islands of Saint-Domingue, Jamaica, and Barbados being cases in point).

231. (A) The rise of northern European mercantile and naval interests in the seventeenth century make statements II and III inaccurate.

232. (D) Sugar, as in the Caribbean, was the initial generator of income in Brazil. Gold became important after its discovery in the Minas Gerais region.

233. (B) Peninsulares were people born in Spain. Creoles were Spaniards born in the New World. Mestizos were a mix of Spanish and Native American.

234. (C) Absolute monarchies would develop by 1750. They were not yet in place in 1450.

235. (B) The Italian Renaissance is credited with creating a transition from Medieval times to the making of early modern Europe. It was mainly a movement that found its expression through the arts, making it more of a cultural change than any of the other choices.

236. (C) Families such as the de' Medici (House of Medici) symbolize this phenomenon.

237. (D) The Spanish monarchy, like all monarchs of the late fifteenth century, was Catholic and sought religious uniformity throughout its kingdom. Be aware that the Huguenots were French Protestants who had yet to exist.

238. (D) In the years 1450 to 1750 the Western societies would process this knowledge to insert themselves as intermediaries in a new web of global trade.

239. (D) This seaward orientation makes it unsurprising that Portuguese mariners took a leading role in oceanic exploration after 1450.

240. (C) This shift in sea supremacy is best represented by the defeat of the Spanish Armada off the coast of England in 1588.

241. (E) Luther's orientation toward biblical, as opposed to Catholic, authority makes his rejection of this element of Christian faith implausible.

242. (E) Remember that he nailed his 95 Theses to a church door in Wittenberg, with the "W" pronounced as a "V," common to the German language.

243. (C) Jesuits were key to Catholic efforts to aggressively spread their brand of Christianity worldwide to counter the rise of new Protestant competitors.

244. (B) While the European population increased overall, growing commercialization of agriculture and enclosure movements that pushed peasants off the land swelled the ranks of proletarians (those who own nothing but their labor power).

245. (B) With time, scientific thinking began to displace religious thinking among educated elites in the West.

246. (C) The Enlightenment in many respects was a logical outgrowth of the Scientific Revolution; as the Scientific Revolution cast doubt on the rule of the church in the realm of ideas, the Enlightenment cast doubt on the rule of kings in the realm of human society.

247. (D) Nicolaus Copernicus was a Polish astronomer whose work disproved the earth as the center of the universe. These findings were later confirmed by Galileo's observations.

248. (C) The Englishman Isaac Newton can be viewed as the father of modern physics. His understanding of motion and gravity held sway until the work of Albert Einstein emerged in the early twentieth century.

249. (A) Locke's formulation of "natural rights" is a key Enlightenment concept.

250. (B) Other civilizations, as a rule, placed greater stock in religion, this being least true of the Chinese.

251. (D) Absolute monarchs, grown more rich and powerful through command of maritime trade and New World colonies, tended to centralize authority at the expense of the lesser aristocracy. The case of French monarchy and Louis XIV is a prime example.

252. **(E)** England stands apart from a trend toward absolute monarchy; patterns of limited monarchy dating back to the rise of Parliament in the twelfth century, and the Magna Carta of the thirteenth century, laid a basis for the emergence of a constitutional and not absolute monarchy in England.

253. **(D)** Parliament gained power to approve taxation and expenditure, also known as the "power of the purse," during the Glorious Revolution of 1689.

254. **(C)** Adam Smith was the foremost spokesman for the interests of a rising British merchant class seeking minimum interference from royal authority in business dealings.

255. **(B)** Divine right was a religious reflection of the rise of absolute monarchy; remember absolute monarchy and Enlightenment philosophy as being in opposition.

256. **(D)** In this arrangement peasants took raw material, often wool, into their cottages and performed labor there to contribute to the production of a finished manufactured product.

257. **(C)** Of the groups listed in the choices, proletarians had the fewest alternatives to factory work.

258. **(E)** Henry VIII famously split from the Catholic church and set up the Anglican church in order to pursue a divorce prohibited by Catholic regulations.

259. **(D)** These patterns are each repeated and amplified as Western maritime empires move to the center of the world economy in the period 1450–1750, integrating the New World into the Old.

260. **(C)** Awareness of this circumstance is key to understanding the move of the West toward the core of a new global economy in the period 1450–1750.

261. **(E)** Multiple factors came into play for this most important "nondecision" in world history.

262. **(C)** These islands off the coast of West Africa were suited for intensive sugar cultivation and were within easy reach of mariners who had yet to cross the Atlantic. Plantations were established in the first half of the fifteenth century by the Portuguese, and that language is still spoken on those islands today.

263. **(D)** Central America, home of the Aztecs, was "integrated" into the world economy after the arrival of Cortez in 1519.

264. **(C)** The Maori people are believed to have arrived in New Zealand sometime before the year 1300.

265. (D) The line, established in 1493 in a treaty signed in the city of Tordesillas in the Valladoid province of Spain, passes through South America in a manner that roughly divides the present-day nation of Brazil from the Spanish-speaking portions of the continent. Even today, Portuguese is the official language in Brazil.

266. (D) Dutch Java became a prototype for European colonization of non-American lands.

267. (D) Magellan himself never made it around the globe, but two of his ships did. He died in the Philippines in 1521.

268. (E) All of the choices are specific contributing factors to the important "power vacuum" that existed circa 1450.

269. (E) While choices **(A), (B),** and **(C)** look tempting, syphilis is a sexually transmitted disease that was introduced to the Europeans upon their arrival to the New World.

270. (A) The Columbian Exchange dramatically increased contact between societies in the Eastern and Western hemispheres. This included diseases, livestock, and crops.

271. (D) In every other body of water listed, the West encountered existing naval and coastal military presences that required sustained campaigns to overcome or with whom Western ships had to coexist.

272. (E) Sugar, tobacco, and coffee all had addictive properties, allowing for these commodities to be very profitable.

273. (C) The Congolese King Afonso's appeals to the Portuguese for the cessation of the slave trade in his territory were rebuffed. Middle Eastern, South Asian, and particularly East Asian civilizations were in a strong position to dictate terms of trade with the West in the period 1450–1750.

274. (D) Being the first to round the Cape of Good Hope and reach the Indian Ocean with the voyages of Vasco da Gama in 1495, the Portuguese followed up by seizing strategic positions at shipping choke points around the Indian Ocean basin soon thereafter.

275. (C) Dutch control of spice production in Java was a huge accomplishment for the Dutch.

276. (D) The shift from the Ming to the Qing is also important because the Ming were the last dynasty to effectively control interaction with the foreign world, particularly the West, and maintain terms advantageous to ruling Chinese elites.

277. (B) Mongol expansion touched major civilizations across the Eurasian landmass, and its collapse opened space for the emergence of new powers, particularly in the Muslim world. Additionally, new Russian and Chinese ruling dynasties emerged in the period following Mongol rule.

278. (C) Safavid Persia has become Iran and is still the center of the Shia branch of Islam today.

279. (D) The original Islamic caliphates reached Spain while the Ottoman Empire did not.

280. (D) Ottoman military forces invading Central Europe laid siege to Vienna (in present-day Austria) twice but failed both times to take the city.

281. (B) Akbar made efforts to reduce the hostility of the Hindu majority of the subcontinent to Muslim rule.

282. (D) Akbar's rule is also known as a time when the status of women was rising. Special market days for women were declared as well, presumably so that women might speak, act, and conduct business more freely without the presence of men.

283. (E) Confucian influence has spread to Korea, Japan, and Southeast Asia but never into the subcontinent. Western missionaries had been met with limited success by 1750 in some Indian coastal areas.

284. (A) New World silver washed across the globe, upsetting regional economies in the sixteenth and seventeenth centuries.

285. (A) By 1750 each of the Muslim empires confronted a world situation where access to foreign trade involved well-armed Western intermediaries.

286. (A) Muslim, Chinese, Japanese, West Africans . . . political leaders in each region tended to ignore threats posed by rising Western power until it was too late and they had been forced into unfavorable trade relations.

287. (E) Lack of clear succession rules have destabilized Muslim communities since the death of Muhammad.

288. (C) The Safavid Empire made determined efforts to expel or convert Sunni and Sufi followers of Islam; the Spanish and Holy Roman Empires ruled territories racked by religious wars coming out of the Protestant Reformation. The Ottoman Empire ruled Palestine, which has been a land of religious diversity since the classical era. The Mughal dynasty was a Muslim minority grafted onto a largely Hindu society in India.

289. (E) Perhaps this choice is true for the Ottoman Empire, but not for the other two.

290. (E) Strong centralized state structures, high population densities, and military sophistication enabled China and Japan in particular to set strict limits on Western contact in this time period.

291. (B) Bullion is another term for precious metals. Westerners had it in increasing amounts because of their control of the New World, and it is the only commodity Western merchants had that East Asian merchants and rulers desired on a consistent basis. Steam engines had yet to be invented, and British shipment of opium into China arose on a mass scale after 1750.

292. (C) While a greater presence was established in Africa, with fewer forts in South Asia and even fewer in East Asia by 1750, as a general rule Westerners were on the scene but not directing state affairs.

293. (A) Isolation was shown by the 1433 withdrawal of the treasure ships. Following Mongol rule in the Yuan dynasty the Ming reinstituted Confucian values, and demographic expansion was caused by availability of New World crops.

294. (C) East Asia has been the most populous region on earth since the classical era, and that is still the case today.

295. (B) The voyages were too much of a break from tradition with too few tangible benefits for Confucian bureaucrats steeped in tradition to embrace.

296. (A) Unlike the Mongols, Manchu rulers relied on Confucian bureaucrats at very high levels of the bureaucracy. Like Mongols, the Manchu held the top posts in government.

297. (E) Regional lords (*daimyo*) converted and led Christianized populations in warfare against each other and uprisings against the imperial center. Christianity had become a mobilizing factor in an ongoing situation of feudal conflict and was targeted as a threat to internal order by the Tokugawa Shogunate.

298. (D) This situation symbolized Eastern control over Western influence, adding a touch of historical irony to its devastation in World War II.

299. (C) The Jesuit order was the leading force in spreading the Catholic faith worldwide as a counteroffensive against the headway Protestant faiths were making in the sixteenth and seventeenth centuries. Refer to question 243.

300. (C) The Philippines were claimed by Magellan for Spain in 1521 and were a key base in the Pacific routes between China and Mexico. Spain held onto the Philippines well after it lost its Latin American holdings in the nineteenth century.

Chapter 4

301. (D) When you hear or see the word *industrial*, think of the word *factory*. All of the other choices were preindustrial motives as well.

302. (C) "Divide and conquer" remained a key tactic of control for colonial powers since the Dutch pioneered it in seventeenth-century Java.

303. (E) These "men on the spot" had considerable latitude in the relations they established with indigenous elites as they penetrated the subcontinent. Preindustrial communication delays meant reports to and instructions from England were many months in transit.

304. (D) The role of the colony in the industrial era is not to be a center of industrial production.

305. (B) Colonial society functioned best when each person knew his or her "place." Traditional hierarchical structures assisted in this arrangement.

306. (A) Colonialists were influenced in many ways by the culture of the "native," but they drew the line at religion in general.

307. (B) Loyal cooperation was more valued than coerced obedience when it came to managers who were often trusted with important administrative tasks.

308. (D) The famine in Bengal flies in the face of claims by British imperialists that their rule banished famine in India.

309. (B) Ritual wife burning was targeted by British colonial officials as a barbaric practice that must be brought to a stop.

310. (D) China and Brazil were not industrial rivals; in fact, the only non-Western nation to gain this status by 1900 was Japan.

311. (D) Major direct military clashes between rival imperialists exploded in the First World War, not before.

312. (B) Independent but influenced by the West were important commonalities of all of these regions.

313. (B) No white minority of any significant size (relative to total population) has ever settled in India.

314. (E) All of the choices capture the mix of divide and conquer, paternalism, and racism that characterized the colonial relationship.

315. (B) Particularly racist notions about the African inability to learn, notoriously prevalent in Belgian rule of the Congo for instance, meant that colonial administrations viewed setting up anything more than rudimentary schooling as a waste of time and resources. Church groups did it out of charity if any Westerners bothered to set up schools at all.

316. (D) Again, the colony was not a place to be industrialized but rather a place that might supply the raw material and might purchase the product.

317. (D) Famously, no Africans were involved in negotiations that, to a large degree, drew political boundaries that remain in place on the continent today.

318. (C) Gandhi was radicalized by racist prohibitions in South Africa that barred him from freely practicing the profession he had studied in London, law.

319. (D) With the revolution starting in Great Britain, it makes sense that it would spread to continental Europe and then the United States.

320. (B) Slavery is exceedingly undemocratic—contrary to the democracy that was being fought for.

321. (A) Looking over the events, we see that the formation of the National Assembly must come first and that the rule of Napoleon must come last.

322. (D) *Declaration of the Rights of Man and Citizen* contained key rights that included liberty, property, security, and resistance to oppression.

323. (D) As the leading element of the Third Estate before the revolution, this group enjoyed a high status after the revolution, an unsurprising outcome.

324. (B) Family ties with the deposed French monarchy and fear of the spread of revolution on the part of neighboring monarchies made imitation or indifference toward the events in France impossible.

325. (C) Records are incomplete but estimates range from 16,000 to 40,000; these numbers pale in comparison with twentieth-century instances of political violence.

326. (E) Sexist practices proved very durable and were codified in the Napoleonic Code.

327. (B) Classical liberal ideas are most closely associated with the interests of the rising middle class and bourgeoisie of nineteenth-century Europe.

328. (A) Conservatives sought to preserve aristocratic privilege as much as possible while radicals sought to improve the status of working people. Refer to question 327.

329. (D) Russian czarism was the strongest monarchy in Europe and successfully insulated its society from Western political trends following Russia's defeat of Napoleon's invasion in 1812.

330. (C) The 1830s saw the Reform Bill in England and Jacksonian democracy in the United States, where voting rights were expanded to new segments of the population.

331. (E) Absolute monarchy can only be said to have existed in Russia, and it was on the defensive even there.

332. (D) Minimum-wage laws were not established until the New Deal era reforms of the 1930s.

333. (E) Locke was a late-seventeenth-century thinker, while the others would make their mark later in history.

334. (D) The U.S. Civil War, a massive resource base, nearly unrestricted immigration, and territorial expansion to the western portion of the North American continent all combined to make the United States a leading industrial power.

335. (A) The United States held on to slavery within its national borders until the Civil War of the 1860s.

336. (C) In particular, the rise of German naval capacity was seen as a threat by the British. It wouldn't be much longer before Germany was involved in two wars.

337. (C) Initial industrialization is often of the "light industrial" variety, focused around textile production. This is greatly different from what industrialization was to become.

338. (C) Business interests associated with liberal politicians generally opposed choices **(A)**, **(B)**, and **(D)**, but radical politicians demanded such reforms. Neither group would have supported a return of monarchy.

339. (A) The thirteen colonies cannot be said to have contained a "peasantry" on anything like the feudal terms that existed in France, while statements I and II were true for both.

340. (C) Workers did not organize what we recognize as unions until after they were brought together into factories and mines by the hundreds and thousands at a time.

341. (D) To oversimplify, Spencer can be viewed perhaps as combining the conclusions of Hobbes (life is "a war of each against all") and Darwin (natural selection) to come to the conclusion that "survival of the fittest" was the proper state for human affairs.

342. (B) Only Latin American nations fit this description.

343. (B) Latin American nations serve as something of a preview of the challenges of post-colonial development the rest of the developing world would face in the post–World War II era. Economic dependency on the West was chief among those challenges.

344. (D) Creole elites aimed for little more change than ejection of the peninsulares; Haiti's revolution showed the risks of slave uprisings for the Creole elites.

345. (D) Conscious of the rhetoric of the French Revolution, enslaved Haitians rose in revolt and achieved independence in 1803.

346. (C) This temporary decapitation of the Spanish Empire opened a window of opportunity for Creole self-government that sparked desires for complete independence.

347. (B) Portugal's king relocated to Brazil and declared it an independent monarchy in 1822. Every other Latin American colony became a republic.

348. (E) For large groups, then, the changes brought by independence were cosmetic, not profound.

349. (C) The year 1800 is a good, round year to imagine the Industrial Revolution gaining real momentum. Patterns of urbanization, factory work, and other items that we recognize to be "industrial" became increasingly prominent after that date.

350. (C) These men were known as *caudillos*, and their interference in politics has become such a pattern that historians speak of a "*caudillo* phenomenon" in Latin American history.

351. (D) In Latin American politics, Centralists tended to be liberal reformers with more ambitious modernization schemes while Federalists tended to be more conservative regional leaders looking to maintain the status quo.

352. (B) Descendants of the Creole elites continued to dominate politics no matter what political party happened to be in power.

353. (C) While the United States proclaimed a Monroe Doctrine opposing any possible "recolonization" of independent Latin American nations, it was the British navy that was the guarantor of security of any form in the Atlantic world of the first half of the nineteenth century.

354. (C) Local manufacturing for internal Latin American markets was difficult to get off the ground because low tariffs made it hard for infant industry to compete with cheaper goods manufactured in Great Britain or elsewhere.

355. (E) By the nineteenth century primary products of industrial production and food-stuffs to feed burgeoning populations in Europe and North America generated the bulk of Latin America's trade relations with the world.

356. (A) The Mexican-American War of the 1840s was a major victory for the United States in that it was able to conquer New Mexico, parts of northern Mexico, and California.

357. (A) This most closely matches a classic liberal political program and describes the Juarez regime that ruled in the mid-nineteenth century.

358. (A) The Mapuche and Auracanian people maintained armed resistance against white incursion into the late nineteenth century.

359. (E) Southern Europeans, Italians in particular, were attracted to Argentina in the decades before and after the turn of the twentieth century—a period of massive emigration to the United States as well. Inexpensive steam ship passage was key.

360. (A) Business interests and modernization have trumped liberal politics many times over in postcolonial societies.

361. (E) Spain's last remaining colonies were lost to the United States in this 1898 conflict.

362. (D) This episode dates from 1903 and occurred under the supervision of U.S. President Theodore Roosevelt.

363. (D) Mesoamerica was the most densely populated region of the New World when Cortez arrived there, and it became Spain's richest colony thanks to the labor of the millions of indigenous people who survived initial disease outbreaks. This dense indigenous population continued to be a force throughout Mexican history as witnessed by the emergence of prominent leaders of indigenous background such as Miguel Hidalgo and Benito Juarez.

364. (C) Yet, by 1914 neither would be formally colonized but both would be reduced to economically dependent relationships with the West.

365. (C) Turkey now occupies the Anatolian peninsula that was the heartland of the Ottoman Empire.

366. (D) This question serves as a useful listing of the Tanzimat reforms.

367. (C) Muhammad Ali's Egypt stands as a case of thwarted industrialization outside the West, contrasting with successful industrialization in Japan and Russia.

368. (D) This waterway was a hugely important shortcut around the African landmass.

369. (E) This trend tends to breed resentment and poverty in the countryside, which can build to unsustainable levels and explode into revolt.

370. (B) China enjoyed a favorable balance of trade during the Qing era all the way up until the advent of the opium trade in the early nineteenth century.

371. (E) Communism would have to wait until the twentieth century to become influential in China.

372. (C) This imperial arrogance causes a stunning lack of awareness of the danger the West would pose.

373. (B) Even in 1800, Chinese industrial capacity surpassed that of the British. For centuries the only commodity the British and other Westerners had that the Chinese desired was silver.

374. (A) In these respects the communist movement that emerged in the 1920s can be seen to be picking up where the Taiping movement of the 1850s and 1860s left off. Ideology was the difference, with the Taiping leaders being gripped by a sinified Christianity while the communist leaders were adhered to a sinified Marxism. Even here similarity persists since both ideologies were Western in origin.

375. (E) The Italians came relatively late to the nineteenth-century race for colonies and limited their ambitions to the African continent.

376. (C) The Tanzimat reforms were an Ottoman Empire initiative while the other four were Chinese movements.

377. (C) China's agricultural and urban heartlands lie roughly in the eastern coastal region between the Yellow and Yangtze rivers.

378. (A) Lin Zexu was an important nineteenth-century Chinese figure; this short primary document that he wrote is worth familiarizing yourself with.

379. (D) This unique hairstyle was a distinguishing and commonplace feature of life in China under the Qing dynasty.

380. (C) The foreign invaders were industrial-powered Western imperialists, not nomadic invaders of roughly the same technical and military capacity, such as the Mongols, who possessed superior organization of existing technologies.

381. (C) The other choices stem from either industrial supremacy pioneered in the West [**(A)** and **(B)**] or the influx of New World products [**(D)** and **(E)**].

382. (B) Both managed to imitate Western developments while maintaining distinctive characteristics.

383. (A) Muslim and Chinese civilizations had a more difficult time taking the lead from outsiders, particularly a civilization such as Western Europe that had been comparatively backward just a few short centuries ago, in their view.

384. (E) Remember that the choice must be incorrect. Czarist rule was highly autocratic and spawned multiple uprisings against it from the 1825 Decembrist uprising to anarchist plots of the 1880s to the 1905 Revolution and the revolutions of 1917.

385. (B) The Crimea is a peninsula protruding down from Ukraine into the Black Sea; it is so warm there it has been a summer vacation spot for centuries.

386. (C) Collectivization of agriculture was not a czarist reform, as it began in 1928 during the Bolshevik era. This invalidates all choices except **(C)**.

387. (A) To be specific, the 1905 Revolution is the difference with regard to the choices provided.

388. (C) Unlike representative assemblies in liberal democracies that controlled government expenditure, the Russian Duma had only advisory powers and, as a result, was an impotent parliamentary body.

389. (D) Japan was able to colonize Korea in 1910 while Russia had yet to carry out a similar move.

390. (C) Commodore Matthew Perry's ships arrived in Tokyo bay in 1853 and demonstrated their weapons. Witnessing this, Japan opened to Western trade soon thereafter.

391. (D) This 1868 event transpired just fifteen short years after Matthew Perry's visit, indicating a highly centralized political culture.

392. (C) Much like the British monarch, the Meiji emperor was more or less a figurehead leader.

393. (C) Western models proceeded on more of a free enterprise or laissez-faire footing while Russia and Japan were more state-directed.

394. (B) Religious westernization would have meant conversion to Christianity; Shinto remained the state religion and maintained its mass following.

395. (E) Japanese war-fighting capacity would be turned against a Western foe again in World War II, but in that case, as we know, Japan did not emerge victorious.

396. (D) In their preindustrial eras all of the European powers listed were still colonial powers. Japanese colonization of Korea and Manchuria occurred after their industrialization drive was under way.

397. (D) Latin American choices should stand out as politically independent, along with Japan and Russia. India should stand out as a colony that would gain independence only after World War II.

398. (E) These "men on the spot" had considerable latitude in the relations they established as they penetrated the subcontinent, since preindustrial communication delays meant direction from England was months in arriving.

399. (D) Perhaps the easiest way to remember this is that units of power, in our day electrical power, are still measured in watts, bearing the stamp of James Watt's discovery of steam power. Thomas Edison invented the light bulb, Eli Whitney the cotton gin, which removed seeds more rapidly from cotton fiber. George Washington Carver was a prolific black American inventor who came up with any number of household and industrial uses for the peanut. George Stephenson was the first individual to attach a steam engine to a rail cart and produce a locomotive.

400. (E) Zapata was a leader of peasants demanding land reform in the movements surrounding the 1910 Mexican Revolution, dating from a period many decades after Latin American nations gained independence. Iturbide was a conservative Creole officer who sided against Spain in Mexican independence struggles after 1810; Miguel de Hidalgo was a Mexican priest who led indigenous and mestizo elements in the independence struggle; Bolivar is associated with leading Andean South America to independence while San Martin led independence fights in Argentina.

Chapter 5

401. (B) By the 1960s Western elites and general populations both accepted decolonization as something of an inevitability; France stands as something of an exception, fighting two bitter wars to maintain colonial holdings, one in Indonesia and the other in Algeria. Statement III is nonetheless mainly false.

402. (B) Liberal democracy fell in Russia, Germany, Italy, and across Eastern Europe in the period between the world wars, appearing to be a failed political arrangement to many. Its resurgence after World War II was reinforced by the emergence of the United States as a superpower.

403. (C) For starters, unlike all the other major combatants, United States factories were never successfully targeted for destruction and so the country emerged from the war with an unparalleled industrial capacity. Add to this the international influence of the U.S. military and cultural (Hollywood) presence and broad outlines of American power can be discerned.

404. (B) The United States committed itself to nuclear retaliation if Cold War allies faced Soviet military assault. Many historians credit this willingness to fight with never needing to—the principle of deterrence.

405. (D) These Cold War–era military alliances faced each other across a dividing line that Winston Churchill famously termed the Iron Curtain. For many decades World War III was expected to be fought between these two alliances.

406. (A) These actions are known to historians as de-Stalinization.

407. (D) Josip Tito's Yugoslavia mounted a more or less independent resistance to Nazi invasion during World War II, liberated itself from fascist occupation, and emerged as an independent socialist state after World War II.

408. (C) Certainly untrue, Soviet Cold War industry was the productive base for one side of the greatest arms race in history.

409. (E) The famous Marshall Plan, named after George Marshall, was an important factor in maintaining Western Europe as part of the liberal democratic and not socialist camp during the early phases of the Cold War.

410. (C) From June 1948 to May 1949 the Royal Air Force and United States Air Force organized flights to provide necessities to the people of West Berlin.

411. (E) Japanese workers are unionized but generally do not strike. They traditionally enjoy lifetime employment at a single firm in a broad social agreement that more or less has maintained labor peace.

412. (B) The two major wars occurred in Korea (1950–1953) and Vietnam (1955–1975), countries located in Asia.

413. (A) Choices I and II are true for both countries. Choice III is true for Korea and false for Vietnam.

414. (C) General Douglas MacArthur famously proposed using tactical nuclear weapons to turn the tide against Chinese communist forces that joined the battle in the Korean War. No prominent U.S. military or civilian official suggested dropping nuclear bombs on Vietnam, in public at least. Refer to question 413 as well.

415. (E) This campaign coincided with drought and crop failures that led to widespread food shortages.

416. (D) To wit, the famous "one-child" policy for urban families.

417. (C) Significant institutional and economic disruption resulted from this campaign that was both launched and dismantled by Mao.

418. (D) It's fair to say that the Chinese Communist Party has put striving for egalitarianism on the proverbial back burner for the time being.

419. (A) Since Deng Xiaoping became leader of the Chinese Communist Party in 1979, China has seen economic but not political reform.

420. (B) This is the defining challenge of postcolonial life.

421. (D) Not that there is a demonstrable connection between the two, if it is to be accepted at all that women's status is improving

422. (A) Patterns of underdevelopment, such as overspecialization in export of a few raw materials or crops set in motion in the colonial era, made achieving such ambitious economic goals a tall order for nationalist leaders.

423. (B) Most developing nations have experienced military rule at some point.

424. (E) Kwame Nkrumah was the leader of the first African nation to gain independence, Ghana, in 1957. The old colonial name used by the British, the Gold Coast, was replaced by Ghana as a reminder of ancient patterns of civilization that predated European colonization.

425. (E) Egypt, like the rest of Africa, still imports most of its durable consumer goods.

426. (E) Caste remains a defining feature of Indian civilization despite decades of (perhaps half-hearted) government efforts to reform it out of existence.

427. (C) The mere fact that the West did not have an influence makes the Iranian Revolution unique in twentieth-century history.

428. (D) Pakistan lost East Pakistan in 1972, which seceded and became the independent nation of Bangladesh.

429. (C) The Organization of Petroleum Exporting Countries (OPEC) fixes oil prices at levels agreed on by the governments of developing countries, not Western consumers.

430. (C) The Nationalist Party that negotiated independence in 1960 ruled an apartheid state where the majority black population could not vote.

431. (B) Steven Biko was an antiapartheid activist in the 1960s and 1970s who was killed while in police custody, while Mandela's involvement can be traced as far back as the 1950s and is forever identified with the twenty-six years he spent in prison while the antiapartheid struggle was carried on by his compatriots outside.

432. (E) Nigeria's petroleum industry is the main force behind its GDP.

433. (B) Be careful not to be too quick to pick choice **(A)**. European elites, particularly Central and Eastern European elites, were traumatized by the Bolshevik seizure of power in Russia, and the first promise of fascist regimes wherever they came to power was to stamp out the communist threat.

434. (C) "Il Duce" was invited to power by the king of Italy after the 1922 "March on Rome."

435. (C) Dating from 1910, the Mexican Revolution predates the next successful revolution of the twentieth century, the Bolshevik Revolution of 1917. The French Revolution dates from 1789 and is therefore not a twentieth-century event while the Chinese (1949) and Iranian (1979) revolutions occurred midcentury and after.

436. (C) The leading role played by mestizo and Indian elements in Mexican politics dates back to the prominence of Miguel de Hidalgo in the 1830s and continued through the era of Benito Juarez in the nineteenth century. In the 1910 revolution this trend was embodied again in the key role played by Emiliano Zapata's largely indigenous peasant-based movement for land reform.

437. (D) The liberal Kerensky regime lasted from the spring to the fall of 1917.

438. **(D)** In popular consciousness it was the communists who could provide peace, land, and bread—not that peace, land, and bread would provide communism.

439. **(D)** Old habits did not meet the socialist ideal but were dependable.

440. **(B)** The Union of Soviet Socialist Republics was made up of these semiautonomous republics.

441. **(D)** Stalin came to power after the death of Lenin in 1924.

442. **(D)** Marxism gave subsequent revolutionary movements the explicit goal of a dictatorship of the proletariat.

443. **(E)** The coal, iron deposits, and timber of Manchuria, as well as the mass markets in China, were an irresistible prize for Japanese imperialists.

444. **(B)** While the Chinese nationalists never fully suspended offensive operations against communist base areas or suspected communist sympathizers between 1927 and the communist victory in 1949, the period after Japan's all-out invasion of China in 1937 prompted some cessation of hostilities between nationalists and communists in pursuit of the common aim of defeating Japanese aggression.

445. **(A)** Statement III is untrue of 1920s economic policy, which tended toward a laissez-faire orientation, and hence ruins choices **(B)**, **(C)**, and **(E)**.

446. **(D)** Mounting agricultural overproduction, rising income inequality, weakening purchasing power among the working classes, rampant stock speculation, and irresponsible extension of credit, among other factors, in the 1920s culminated in the stock market crash of 1929. Banks were unable to honor withdrawals and stopped most lending, prompting widespread shutdowns of industrial production. This led to waves of layoffs and rising unemployment that were somewhat ameliorated by FDR's New Deal. Across the industrialized West it was the Second World War and preparation for it that reversed the economic catastrophe of the Great Depression.

447. **(B)** This advantage of colonial holdings was established during late-nineteenth-century economic downturns.

448. **(C)** The other nations on the list evolved fascist regimes of some sort.

449. **(C)** *Lebensraum* translates roughly to "living room." German people had settled in pockets across Slavic Eastern Europe and even into Central Asia by the nineteenth century; in his 1925 book *Mein Kampf* Hitler proposed a campaign to make all these eastern lands a part of a "Greater Germany" where the existing populations would be subjugated and made to serve the interests of the German people.

450. (C) *Mein Kampf* ("My Struggle") was published in 1925 and made Hitler's broad goals for the Third Reich plain for the world to see.

451. (C) With key Italian and German assistance, Franco's fascist forces emerged victorious in the Spanish Civil War; Germany and Japan lost World War II, of course.

452. (B) Statement III ruins choices **(C)**, **(D)**, and **(E)** since colonialism ended in the nineteenth century. Both I and II are accurate as the world witnessed the collapse of the Chilean copper industry and the rise of corporatist dictatorial regimes (such as the Vargas regime in Brazil and the Peron regime in Argentina).

453. (E) Fascism involves very tight government supervision of not only the political but also the economic life of a nation. Laissez-faire means just the opposite.

454. (C) Japan's more homogeneous ethnic makeup made events like Kristallnacht (Crystal Night/Night of the Broken Glass), an anti-Jewish movement, a nonissue there.

455. (A) Both regimes are considered to be fascist.

456. (E) Soviet development (as with many developments until recent decades) is not known for environmental concern.

457. (C) *Glasnost* is a Russian term for the economic reforms that allowed for more private ownership, and *perestroika* translates to a new "openness" in politics that allowed for more public criticism of Soviet government and society. Soviet socialism could not survive more than five or six years of these policies.

458. (A) Vast resources inside the USSR, plus access to that of satellite Eastern European nations, make statement III untrue. Since both statements I and II are true, choice **(A)** is best.

459. (E) The Castro dictatorship, by all appearances, is still firmly ensconced in power.

460. (D) This process has accelerated since the dissolution of the Soviet system and the reversion of the entire world economy toward a model with the United States at its center.

461. (A) Vast areas of Africa and Asia will skip the entire "land line" phase of communications development and move right into mobile technologies.

462. (D) Western interests are still central in the world economy but are no longer accompanied by Western flags of colonialism.

463. (C) Major wars in Iraq and Afghanistan have been supplemented by air strikes in Pakistan, Yemen, and Somalia. Most of this action has been taken after September 11 as part of a "War on Terror."

464. (C) While some of the hijackers were United Arab Emirate, Lebanese, and Egyptian, the vast majority of the hijackers were Saudi Arabian.

465. (C) They serve as a preview for the challenges of postcolonial development in a world economy with the West at its economic core.

466. (B) The Bay of Pigs invasion of Cuban exiles was a failure, despite U.S. equipment and air support.

467. (E) Cuba's colonial heritage left it overly dependent on sugar production. The United States imposed a blockade of trade with Cuba soon after 1959, leaving Cuba with few trading partners but the Soviets. Since the 1990 collapse of the USSR, Cuba has struggled for economic growth in the context of this blockade.

468. (E) Cuban socialism has provided choices **(A)** through **(D)**, but Cuban people cannot leave the island easily if they do not like it there.

469. (B) This variant of Catholicism focuses on biblical passages that speak of Jesus' mission to bring justice to this world, and emerged in Latin America in the 1950s and 1960s.

470. (B) The pattern of migration to the cities is, perhaps, surprising to North Americans, but true.

471. (B) This is a unique feature of Mexico in modern Latin American history.

472. (E) This war in the winter of 1989–1990 was launched by the George H. W. Bush administration to remove Manuel Noriega from power in Panama.

473. (A) The days of old-style colonialism were finished by the second half of the twentieth century.

474. (C) Central America, including Mexico, is regarded as part of the North American continent, and NAFTA, short for the North American Free Trade Agreement, was signed in 1994 under the Clinton administration.

475. (C) These events appear in the correct chronology in choice **(C)**, and the experiences of these years shaped subsequent twentieth-century developments in each region of the globe. Before this "Age of Catastrophe," Africa and Asia remained colonized and communists had not seized power anywhere. By 1945 the stage was set for a wave of independence in the colonies and a worldwide confrontation between communist and liberal democratic states, the Cold War, that would last for most of the rest of the century.

476. (A) Considering the broad sweep of the twentieth century, this is the most accurate choice.

477. (E) Political independence for India had to wait for the aftermath of World War II.

478. (B) In South Africa, apartheid lasted until the 1990s.

479. (C) The economic and military rise of Germany was the main factor that upset the balance of European power in place since the defeat of Napoleon and the Congress of Vienna.

480. (E) Nowhere in 1914 did communists command the economic or state power necessary to mount operations on the scale of world war.

481. (C) Russia's turning from czarism to communism is a classic case of unforeseen outcomes in history.

482. (D) Power was transferred from colonial elites to the local elites, a pattern established in Latin American independence movements of the nineteenth century.

483. (C) Liberal democracies tend to go into something of a "survival mode" in wartime and employ more authoritarian methods.

484. (C) Total war's mobilization of all of a society's resources, including the labor of women, made longstanding demands by feminists of the right to vote much more difficult to deny. If women could play key roles in the economic life of the nation at its hour of greatest need, it became difficult to justify keeping women from playing a role in the political life of the nation as well.

485. (C) Czechoslovakia was carved from the old Austro-Hungarian Empire, like much of Central and Eastern Europe is today.

486. (D) While representatives of colonized peoples were in attendance at Versailles, the entire proceedings had the tone of being strictly run by a "white man's club" led by the French, British, and U.S. delegations. In particular, Japanese territorial ambitions in East Asia were thwarted.

487. (B) The rhetoric of self-determination of nations that emerged after World War I was limited in practice to new nations in Eastern Europe.

488. (C) India's large educated middle class by colonial standards provided a firm base for the early emergence of an independence movement.

489. (D) Anti-Ottoman sentiment and organization dates from the closing decades of the nineteenth century.

490. (D) This support came to be known as the Balfour Declaration.

491. (C) The newly installed Bolshevik regime negotiated an immediate withdrawal from the fighting.

492. (C) German fascists moved into Austria, Japanese fascists moved into China, Italian fascists moved into Ethiopia, and homegrown fascists took over in Spain.

493. (D) While the fighter plane skirmishes of World War I were limited in scope, they nonetheless are the only choice on the list that existed prior to World War II.

494. (E) Total war mobilizes the full military, industrial, institutional, and intellectual resources of a society for victory in a life-or-death struggle, and treats enemy societies, not just military forces, as war-making entities as well. The distinction between military and civilian targets is blurred in total war.

495. (C) The Soviet Union put up the stiffest resistance to Nazi invasion of any European nation with the possible exception of Yugoslavia. Many people claim that the weather conditions in Russia were partly responsible for this slowdown.

496. (B) While escape in handfuls occurred at many camps, an entire extermination camp, Sobibor, was shut down by the Nazis after an October 1943 mass escape.

497. (E) While the other arguments are legitimate points of debate, nobody argues that U.S. policy makers had peaceful atomic energy in mind when they dropped nuclear weapons on Hiroshima and Nagasaki.

498. (B) The violence of the partition of India and Pakistan had long-term causes dating back to the period of British colonial rule and further back to Hindu resentment of Muslim domination in the Mughal era.

499. (D) European settler minorities had lived in the colonies for generations by the 1960s, occupied high rank in society, and were numerous enough to marshal the resources to put up stiff resistance to decolonization.

500. (C) Broad agreement on the establishment of Israel (outside the Arab world) stemmed from the uniquely horrific experience of European Jewry among the many horrors of the Second World War.